EQUIDIST
VOCES EQUIDISTANTES

EQUIDISTANT VOICES

For many writers who live away from their country of birth, and expressly when their first language is not the language spoken in their adoptive country, it is doubly difficult to get their creative work fully acknowledged. Not only may the links with their own cultural origins and influences become lessened or even lost, but late arrival on foreign soil could make their integration into a new cultural setting extremely challenging. The present anthology –and there are certainly no claims that it is incontestable in any way– aims to uphold the literary output from Latin American poets by developing their creative work in the UK. Our purpose is to disseminate their work both in their countries of origin and, with this bilingual edition, in the English-speaking world. Finally, the book also includes an extensive study
on the translation of contemporary Latin American poetry into English.

VOCES EQUIDISTANTES

Para muchos escritores, vivir en un país diferente al de su nacimiento, más aún cuando no se comparte la lengua, representa una doble dificultad en el reconocimiento de su obra: por un lado, se suele truncar prematuramente la relación con el campo cultural de origen y sus instituciones; por el otro, se llega tardíamente a un campo cultural nuevo en el que resulta muy complicado integrarse. Esta antología – sin pretensiones de infalibilidad - se propone recuperar esas voces poéticas latinoamericanas que actualmente desarrollan su obra creativa en el Reino Unido, para darlas a conocer en sus países natales.
El volumen incluye un amplio estudio sobre la traducción al inglés
de la poesía latinoamericana contemporánea.

Latin American Poets in the UK
Poetas latinoamericanos en el Reino Unido

Equidistant voices
Voces equidistantes

POETRY / *POESÍA*

Selection and Introductory Study
Selección y estudio introductorio
Enrique D. Zattara

Translation
Traducción
Isabel del Rio

© 2023, **Enrique D. Zattara**
Portada: **Oscar Grillo**

ISBN: 979-8379253455

© Edition: 2023,
EDICIONES EQUIDISTANCIAS,
EL OJO DE LA CULTURA,
FRIENDS OF ALICE PUBLISHING

INTRODUCTION

In many Latin America countries, the word *London* immediately stirs thoughts of the world of finance, the cradle of free trade and globalisation. Indeed, London is unquestionably all these things. Alongside New York, the UK capital is a veritable symbol and emblem of the changes resulting from technological advancements, the supremacy of markets, and the impact of global influence.

But London is also a truly fascinating city, a permanent crossroads between the historic past and the avant-garde. It is undoubtedly the setting where multiculturalism peaks to summits which no other urban landscape can likely reach. Ultimately, London inspires adventures both existential and intellectual well above other cities, the reasons for which may not be altogether clear but are very much there.

Throughout history there have been countless artists and writers who lived and worked in London, whether for a short period or on a permanent basis. Perhaps this was because the city was a major hub in terms of culture, but then one cannot help but fall in love with London. In the case of Latin American writers and artists, this influx has grown exponentially in the last few decades, despite any difficulties arising from learning the English language itself. Such influx is the result of both an increasing interest in acquiring diverse experiences and involvements, and the ease of travel between distant parts of our planet.

Some of these writers now belong to the history of literature, whether universal or in their countries of origin, and as expected they have been translated into English and into many other languages. Other writers have become integrated into the British literary scene and write (or wrote) in both languages. Lastly, there are others who continue to write in Spanish.

Recently, in collaboration with the Cervantes Institute in London we organised a permanent series of conferences and discussions on Latin American writers who have not yet attained the necessary recognition by the British public and critics. As part of this series, in 2019 we organised a discussion panel to publicise the many important and accomplished women poets who appeared in the Latin American literary scene during the second half of the 20th century, specifically those born approximately between 1920 and 1970. Subsequently, I carried out further research, solely for my personal interest, regarding their poetry and, particularly, the translation of their work.

My research took place mostly at London's Poetry Library (located on the 5th floor of the Royal Festival Hall, the most significant cultural venue in London). And it was in the course of my research work that I made an intriguing discovery. There it was, glaring at me: a small bilingual book published in 1988, with the title *Antología de los poetas latinoamericanos en Londres*. It had been published by a hitherto unknown collective with the name of "Grupo de Escritores Latinamericanos en Londres". I had not heard of the group before (in any case, I had arrived in London in 2015); in all likelihood, this group no longer existed (and thirty years had elapsed since its creation). The book included eleven authors of different nationalities, and the translations into English were either by the poets themselves or by translators whom I do not know; it also included a preamble by Roberto Rivera-Reyes, a Chilean writer who, it appears, headed the group.

Of all the members of the group I knew only two of them, the Mexican poet Pedro Serrano (born in Canada), who at present edits the major literary magazine "El Periódico de Poesía" and whom I had interviewed a couple of years earlier when he visited London (he no longer lives in London but in Mexico); and the Chilean poet, María Eugenia Bravo Calderara, who still lives in London, and who is included in the present anthology. To keep their memory alive, here are the names of the other members of that group: Alfredo Cordal (who died in 2022), Enrique Parada, Roberto Rivera-Reyes and Jorge Salgado Rocha (**Chile**); Edgardo Durán Restrepo and Ricardo García Curbelo (**Colombia**); Carlos Góngora (**Mexico**); Sergio Regules (**Uruguay**); and Pedro Sarduy (**Cuba**).

Unearthing this compact book from the 1980s inspired me to expand my initial undertaking, and I thought that perhaps I should try to recreate what had been done thirty years earlier, particularly as in all likelihood there were now many more Latin American nationals living and writing poetry in London, including myself; and of course, not only in London but in other UK cities. In practical terms, such is the origin of the present book. It was a publishing proposal that we shared with the British-Spanish poet and translator, Isabel del Rio, who would translate the book into English (both this introduction and the selected poems). Thus, the book would be a bilingual edition under the auspices of several independent publishing imprints (Equidistancias, Ojo de la Cultura, Friends of Alice Publishing). Regrettably, the Covid 19 pandemic at the beginning of 2020 disrupted the expected development of the project. Initially the book was published in 2022 by the new publishers **equidistancias** in Buenos Aires, but only in its original version in Castilian. And now, in 2023, the book has finally been published as a bilingual edition.

Before discussing the book itself, it would be useful to talk briefly about the research process with which this whole project began, and also comment on the background references and expressly the translations that were available in London regarding the work by contemporary Latin American poets beyond renowned poets like Neruda, Vallejo, Guillén, Mistral and others from previous generations.

Latin American Poetry in Translation

Latin American poetry played an active role in the avant-garde movements of the first part of the 20th century. English-speakers undoubtedly had access to many of the most noteworthy writers. However, there were not many translations of those Latin American poets who came after Neruda, let alone was their work disseminated in the UK or within an academic context. Back in 1967, Penguin had published *Latin American Writing Today*, a bilingual collection of thirty-two 20th century writers, edited by J.M. Cohen; it included 18 poets, as well as other writers such as Borges or Benedetti who were not embraced as poets but as fiction writers. It is important to note, not so much anecdotally but because of its significance considering the criteria in the world of publishing back then, that only two women were included, the Chilean Gabriela Mistral (awarded the Nobel Prize in Literature in 1945) and the Mexican Rosario Castellanos. As to be expected, the book comprised work by Vallejo, Neruda, Parra and Octavio Paz, but also incorporated new names such as Alí Chumacero, Alberto Girri, Vinicius de Moraes, Joao Cabral de Melo Neto, Jaime Sabines, Marco Antonio Montes de Oca, Pablo Fernández, Enrique Lihn and José Emilio Pacheco.

Shortly afterwards, another anthology was published in the UK: *The Penguin Book of Latin American Verse*. Edited by E. Caracciolo-Trejo and published in 1971, the book includes an introductory essay by Henry Gifford, and showcases both original poems and their translation into English. When the book was published, the most contemporary authors were Edgar Bailey, Alberto Girri and Raúl Gustavo Aguirre (**Argentina**); Alvaro Mutis (**Colombia**); Marco Antonio Montes de Oca, José Emilio Pacheco and Jaime Sabines (**Mexico**); Roberto Fernández Retamar and Pablo Fernández (**Cuba**); Ernesto Cardenal (**Nicaragua**); Carlos Belli (**Peru**); Idea Vilariño (**Uruguay**); and Rafael Cadenas (**Venezuela**). All eighty poets included in this anthology were born between the 1920s and 1930s; only four women writers were included.

We must also mention *Another Republic: 17 European and South American Writers*, published in 1976 by Ecco Press in New York, and edited by Charles Simic and Mark Strand. At present it is extremely difficult to get hold of a copy of this book, even with today's advanced technology.

In 1977, the New York publishers Alfred A. Knopf launched a book edited by the Uruguayan critic Emir Rodríguez Monegal. The title was *The Borzoi Anthology of Latin American Literature*, which aimed to encompass the then current Latin American literary canon in two volumes; chapter 11 of its second volume is dedicated to *Twenty Spanish American Poets*, which comprises the generation of poets that came after Borges, Paz, Neruda, etc. Included are Alberto Girri, César Fernández Moreno (the son of another celebrated poet, Baldomero Fernández Moreno), Roberto Juarroz and Juan Gelman (**Argentina**); Ali Chumacero, Jaime Sabines, Homero Aridjis and José Emilio Pacheco (**Mexico**); Idea Vilariño (**Uruguay**); Cintio Vitier, Fayad Jamis, Pablo Fernández and Heberto Padilla (**Cuba**); Ernesto Cardenal (**Nicaragua**); Blanca Varela, Carlos Germán Belli, Javier Heraud and Antonio Cisneros (**Peru**); Enrique Lihn (**Chile**); and Guillermo Sucre (**Venezuela**). It is important to point out that the book included only two women out of twenty writers, so there was an improvement on previous selections. Also, five Brazilian poets were included (though no women writers). The book solely comprises the English translation of the poems, and no original texts were provided.

The flourishing of anti-capitalist utopias reached their maximum expression with the Cuban Revolution, and some poetic circles at the time echoed the new stance taken by an important number of Latin American authors who declared themselves committed to the liberation struggle against US imperialism, with many of them taking part in various conflicts and even participating in guerrilla warfare. In the 1960s and 1970s, the popularity of Latin American guerrillas and their politically committed poets attracted the attention of English-speaking university students. This led to a number of poetry collections being published, the first of which was: *Our Word: Guerrilla Poems from Latin America*, translated by Edward Dorn and Gordon Brotherstone, published in the US in 1968.

Another book, which became the best-known collection of Latin American poetry at the time, was *Latin American Revolutionary Poetry*, published in 1974 in New York, with translations by Roberto Márquez; this is a bilingual edition, and it features not only the most recent generation of political and social poets, but also its precursors, as is the case the legendary Cuban poet Nicolás Guillén, and poets from a younger generation such as Roberto Fernández Retamar, Nancy Morejón and Daniel Fernández Chericián. Among the poets from Argentina, the book reclaims Enrique Molina, and features Juan Gelman and Víctor García Robles. And among the poets from the previous generation, the book includes Thiago de Melo (**Brazil**), Pedro Mir (**Dominican Republic**), Jorge Enrique Adoum (**Ecuador**), René Depestre (**Haiti**), Edmundo Aray (**Venezuela**), and Ernesto Cardenal (**Nicaragua**); among the younger poets, it includes Pedro Shimosa (**Bolivia**); Enrique Lihn (**Chile**); Roque Dalton (**El Salvador**); Otto Castillo and Marco Antonio Flores (**Guatemala**); Juan Bañuelos (**Mexico**), Antonio Cisneros, Arturo Corcuera and Javier Heraud (**Peru**); Pedro Pietri, Iván Silén and Iris Zavala (**Puerto Rico**); and Mario Benedetti and Carlos María Gutiérrez (**Uruguay**).

In a similar fashion, Pulp Press in Vancouver published *A fist and the letter. Revolutionary Poems of Latin America*, in 1977. This is a bilingual edition, with translations by Roger Prentice and John Kirk, with poems by twenty politically committed poets. Here again we find Cardenal, Dalton, Depestre, Fernández Retamar and Guillén. This book also includes work by Roberto Armijo and Álvaro Menéndez Leal (**El Salvador**); Alejandro Romualdo and Winston Orrillo (**Peru**); Cristina Peri Rossi (**Uruguay**); Julio Huasi (**Argentina**); Omar Lara (**Chile**); and José Martínez Matos, Manuel Navarro Luna, Regino Pedroso, Ricardo Roa (who for many years was Foreign Secretary in Fidel Castro's government) and the popular singer-songwriters Carlos Puebla and Silvio Rodríguez (**Cuba**).

Women in Latin American Poetry

Well before the surge in the recognition of women's role in writing, an anthology of Latin American female writers was published in 1978 in the US. Edited by Nora Weizer, the title of the book was *Open the sun*. It included writers whose main body of work had appeared in the first half of the 20th century, though more contemporary authors were also featured. Such was the case of Rosario Castellanos (**Mexico**); Olga Orozco and Alejandra Pizarnik (**Argentina**); Eunice Odio (**Costa Rica**); Amanda Berenguer, Cristina Meneghetti and Nancy Bacelo (**Uruguay**); Blanca Varela (**Peru**); Ola Elena Mattei (**Puerto Rico**); Belkis Cuza Malé (**Cuba**); and several Nicaraguan poets, such as Gioconda Belli, an obvious addition to the book, and Rosario Murillo, who at present is the Vice-President of Nicaragua.

From then on, it would be Chilean poet Marjorie Agosín (born in 1955), professor at Wellesley College in Maryland, US, who would address further the subject of Latin American women writers. In 1987, Agosín published *The renewal of the visión (Voice of Latin American Women Poets 1940-1980)*. The book had no imprint and was published in collaboration with Cola Franzen in Nottingham, UK; it included poems in translation (into English) but not the original versions in Castilian. Twenty-three poets were featured (presumably born between the 1940s and the 1980s), although several of them in fact were born well before those decades, as in the case of Chilean Violeta Parra (born in 1917), the Mexican Rosario Castellanos (1925) and the Peruvian Blanca Varela (1926). Other poets highlighted in the book were born after 1930: Julia Álvarez (**Dominican Republic**); Alicia Borinsky, Luisa Futoransky and Alejandra Pizarnik (**Argentina**); Cecilia Bustamante (**Peru**); Ana Castillo and Isabel Fraire (**Mexico**); Belkis Cuza Malé and Nancy Morejón (**Cuba**); Myriam Díaz-Diocaretz, Delia Domínguez and Cecilia Vicuña (**Chile**); Rosario Ferré, Rosario Morales and Luz María Umpierre (**Puerto Rico**); Alaide Foppa (**Guatemala**); Rosita Kalina and Eunice Odio (**Costa Rica**); Cristina Peri Rossi (**Uruguay**); and Adelia Prado (**Brazil**).

In 1994, Agosín would publish another exceptional anthology *These are not sweet girls: Poetry by Latin American Women* (White Pine Press, Fredonia, New York). The book is a compilation of poems by fifty-two Latin American women writers. The selection criteria are somewhat subjective, as the texts are grouped according to thematic and stylistic considerations. Although most of the book includes poets who produced their work in the second half of the 20th century, it also includes, rather arbitrarily in my view, more traditional writers like the Argentinian Alfonsina Storni, the Chilean Gabriela Mistral or the Honduran Clementina Suárez.

This book comprises translations by thirty-seven translators, though not the original poems. It has the following sections: "Like the magic glow of paradise", "These are not sweet girls", "Close to me", "Silence that can be heard", "The moon's cadaver", "Gestures from my window" and "To be seventeen again" (this last section embraces the work of popular singer-songwriters whose work is rooted in poetry, as is the case of Violeta Parra; the book leaves out others who are equally prominent, undeservedly in my view).

Herewith the inventory of the poets included in the book: Alfonsina Storni, Alejandra Pizarnik and Mercedes Roffé (**Argentina**); Perla Schwartz, Rosario Castellanos, Coral Bracho, Pita Amor and Elsa Cross (**Mexico**); Gabriela Mistral, Emma Sepúlveda-Pulvireti, Belinda Zubicueta Carmona, Alicia Galaz Vivar, Paz Molina, Teresa Calderón, Cecilia Vicuña, Violeta Parra, and also the editor of the book, Marjorie Agosín (**Chile**); Adelia Prado (**Brazil**); Magda Portal, Laura Riesco and Giovanna Pollarolo (**Peru**); Delmira Agustini, Clara Silva, Amanda Berenguer, Idea Vilariño and Cristina Peri Rossi (**Uruguay**); Yolanda Bedregal and Blanca Wiehütcher (**Bolivia**); Rosario Ferré, Olga Nolla, Masta Arrilaga, Giannina Braschi and Julia de Burgos (**Puerto Rico**); Rosita Kalina, Eunice Odio, Ana Istarú and Carmen Naranjo (**Costa Rica**); Dulce María Lyonaz, Carlota Caulfield, Belkis Cuza Malé, Magali Alabau and Nancy Morejón (**Cuba**); Jeanette Miller, Chiqui Vicioso and Aída Cartagena de Portalatin (**Dominican Republic**); Gioconda Belli and Claribel Alegría (**Nicaragua**); Ana María Rodas, Alaide Foppa and Romelia Alarcón (**Guatemala**); Clementina Suárez (**Honduras**); Anabel Torres (**Colombia**); and Fanny Carrión de Fierro (**Ecuador**). This may not appear to be a fair selection, but it undoubtedly merits recognition because of the extensive amount of work involved in compiling and translating the poems.

In 1984 and before Agosín's book, there was another anthology of Latin American women poets, though I have been unable to locate a copy. The title was *Woman Who Has Sprouted Wings: Poems by Contemporary Latin American Women Poets.* Edited by Mary Crow, it was a bilingual edition and was published by Latin American Literary Review Press, in the US. It comprised fourteen women poets born in the 1930's, except for Rosario Castellanos, Claribel Alegría and Raquel Jodorowsky, who were born in the previous decade.

Most recent translations

The next milestone in our research is a lavish anthology published in 1996 by University of Texas Press, in Austin. Edited by Stephen Tapscott, the title of the book is *Twentieth-Century Latin American Poetry*. This bilingual edition aims to include all 20th century poets, both men and women, beginning with the more traditional poets like José Martí and Rubén Darío. It includes eighty authors, several of them from the period we are discussing, i.e. those who came after the generation of Octavio Paz, Nicanor Parra or even Gonzalo Rojas. Specifically, they include Olga Orozco, Eunice Odio, Álvaro Mutis, Claribel Alegría, Roberto Juarroz, Jaime Sabines, Carlos Germán Belli, Enrique Lihn, Juan Gelman, Ferreira Gullar, Heberto Padilla, Gabriel Zaid, Roque Dalton, Adelia Prado, Jorge Teillier, Alejandra Pizarnik, Oscar Hahn, José Emilio Pacheco, Homero Aridjis, Antonio Cisneros, Nancy Morejón, Octavio Armand, Raúl Zurita and Marjorie Agosín (it is worth noting that Ernesto "Che" Guevara is included in this list of poets).

In 2000, Oxford University Press published a collection of short essays by Professor William Rowe, of Birkbeck College. The title of the book is *Poets of Contemporary Latin America (History and the Inner Life).* The essays include translated sections from the work of the various selected poets, who are halfway between the generation of Neruda and Vallejo and more contemporary poets, including Nicanor Parra (**Chile**), Ernesto Cardenal (**Nicaragua**), Gonzalo Rojas (**Chile**), Jorge Eduardo Eielson (**Peru**), Juan L. Ortiz (**Argentina**), Ana Enriqueta Terán (**Venezuela**), Raúl Zurita (**Chile**) and Carmen Ollé (**Peru**).

The publication of an unusual anthology in 2007 is also worth mentioning. With the title *Literary Amazonia*, the book incorporated –and asserted as a distinct literary group– several authors from the extensive rainforest area in the Amazon Basin, which incorporates a large section of Brazil and territories of other nations such as Bolivia, Paraguay, Peru, Colombia, Ecuador and Venezuela, as well as the territories of the three Guianas, (Guyana, which acquired its independence from Britain in 1975; Suriname, which acquired its independence from the Netherlands in 1975; and French Guiana, which remains a French overseas territory). The book was compiled by the writer Nicomedes Suárez-Araúz, who was born in Beni, in the Bolivian Amazonia, and who also penned the long introduction of the book asserting the identity connecting all writers from this geographical area. The book was published by University Florida Press, and its poetry section includes poems by twenty-three authors, ranging from Raúl Otero

Reiche (born in 1906) to Yenny Muruy Andoque (born in 1969), as well as Thiago de Mello (**Brazil**), who is generally the only Brazilian poet mentioned in other anthologies.

In 2009, Oxford University Press published *The Oxford Book of Latin American Poetry*, in New York. The book was edited by the Chilean poet Cecilia Vicuña and Professor Ernesto Livon-Grosman, from Argentina. This is an invaluable bilingual anthology featuring over 120 poets from the American subcontinent, including several authors writing in indigenous languages. The book also includes several well-known 'experimental' poets whose work features elements that are extrinsic to writing, such as spatiality and various other resources (a clear example are the poems by Vicuña herself). In my view, this work is indispensable reading not only for English-speaking lovers of poetry, but also for Spanish-speakers, as it offers a truly comprehensive selection of poets, including those from more recent generations as well as poets from Brazil (generally excluded because of their being Portuguese-speakers).

I think it would be fair to mention the long list of writers included in the book according to their country of origin (this classification may be useful to future researchers on the subject); nonetheless, readers may wish to skip the next section.

Argentina: Olga Orozco, Gyula Kosice, Francisco Madariaga, Leónidas Lamborghini, Edgardo Vigo, Juan Gelman, Lorenzo Ramos, Antonio Martínez, Susana Thenon, Alejandra Pizarnik, Osvaldo Lamborghini, Arturo Carrera, Néstor Perlongher, Emeterio Cerro, Jorge Perednik, Juan L. Ortiz. **Mexico:** Loxa Jiménez López, María Fernández Kokov, Tonik Nibak, Cristina Rivera Garza, Juan Gregorio Regino, José Gorostiza, Gerardo Deniz, Isabel Fraire, Sergio Mondragón, Gloria Gerwitz, Coral Bracho, Myrian Moscone, Xunka Ut'ntz'Ni. **Brazil:** Josely Vianna Baptista, Wilson Bueno, Paulo Leminski, Augusto De Campos, Haroldo De Campos, Decio Pignatari. **Uruguay:** Idea Vilariño. **Chile:** Pablo de Rokha, Cecilia Meireles, Enrique Lihn, Aurelio Frez, Oscar Hahn, Juan Luis Martínez, Soledad Fariña, Cecilia Vicuña, Raúl Zurita, Elvira Hernández, Elikura Chihuailof. **Guatemala:** Humberto A'Kabal. **Cuba:** Reina María Rodríguez, José Kozer. **Bolivia:** Jaime Sanz. **Venezuela:** Juan Sánchez Peláez, Eugenio Montejo, Alfredo Silva Estrada. **Nicaragua:** Ernesto Cardenal, Carlos Martínez Rivas, Daisy Zamora. **El Salvador:** Roque Dalton. **Peru:** Jorge Eduardo Eielson, Blanca Varela, Carlos Germán Belli, Rodolfo Hinostroza, Antonio Cisneros. **Colombia:** María Mercedes Carranza, Jaime Jaramillo Escobar. May we just point out that there are twenty-one women and forty-three men in the above list.

Another colossal effort is *The FSG book of Twentieth-century Latin American Poetry*, which was published in 2011 by the New York publishers Farrar, Straus & Giroux. A bilingual book of almost 80 pages, it has been carefully edited by Professor Ilan Stavans, of Amherst College. Among the translators involved in the project, we must mention Samuel Beckett and Ursula K. Le Guin. The book obviously includes the more traditional writers like Rubén Darío and José Martí, as well as the best-known authors from the poetry avant-garde of the first part of the 20th century. The second half of the book is an anthology of poets born from 1920 onwards (in other words, poets to whom we have dedicated our brief bibliographical research). Thus, the book includes, in chronological order, poems by Mario Benedetti, Joao Cabral de Melo, Olga Orozco, Álvaro Mutis, Claribel Alegría, Ernesto Cardenal, Roberto Juarróz, Rosario Castellanos, Jaime Sabines, Blanca Varela, Enrique Lihn, Juan Gelman, Heberto Padilla, Roque Dalton, Adélia Prado, Jorge Teillier, Alejandra Pizarnik, Oscar Hahn, José Emilio Pacheco, Homero Aridjis, José Kozer, Antonio Cisneros, Gloria Gervitz, Nancy Morejón, Paulo Leminski, Elsa Cross, Natalio Hernández Xocoyotzin, Darío Jaramillo, Víctor de la Cruz, David Huerta, Alberto Blanco, Coral Bracho, María Negroni, Raúl Zurita, Humberto Ak'abal, Elicura Chihuailaf, Pura López Colomé, Roberto Bolaño, Fabio Morábito, Giannina Braschi, Myriam Moscona, María Baranda, Odi González and Juan Gregorio Regino. It should be noted that some of the above poets write in indigenous languages.

In 2014, the Chilean poet Raúl Zurita produced another literary canon of Latin American writers aimed at English-speaking readers. The title is *Pinholes in the night (Essential Poems from Latin America)*, published by Copper Canyon Press, in Washington. The book includes nineteen 20th century poets, and the translator is Forrest Gander. The editor's criteria are somewhat uncommon, as the literary landscape that the book encapsulates includes fiction writers (although the only fictional story in the book is "¿No oyes ladrar los perros?" from *El llano en llamas* by Juan Rulfo). The book mostly features rather lengthy poems (even the complete version of the seven cantos of *Altazor* by Vicente Huidobro). Zurita keeps to the more traditional poets such as Gabriela Mistral, Huidobro, Vallejo, Borges, Neruda, Nicanor Parra (he does however include the Chilean Pablo de Rokha, an uncommon choice even though he is a great poet). From later generations (as well as oddly including Rulfo), Zurita selects poets like Gonzalo Rojas and Gonzalo Millán (**Chile**); Antonio Cisneros and José Watanabe (**Peru**); Jaime Sabines (**Mexico**); Ernesto Cardenal (**Nicaragua**); Idea Vilariño (**Uruguay**); Juan Gelman, Héctor Viel Temperley and Alejandra Pizarnik (**Argentina**).

Indisputably, the most comprehensive anthology of contemporary Latin American poetry was published in the UK in 2016, with the title *The other tiger, Recent Poetry from Latin America* (Seren Books, Wales). The book was compiled and translated by Richard Gwyn. Unlike previous anthologies, the book opens with poets born in the 1950's; in other words, most of the featured poets are still writing today (in fact, all of them were alive when the book was published; in the case of Watanabe and Bolaño, also born in the 1950's, they were excluded from this anthology as they had already died). In total, this 400-page book includes the work of ninety-six poets writing in many different styles. It should be noted that the selection was based on the poems rather than on the poets themselves, with some of the poets included several times throughout the book.

The title of the book, *El otro tigre*, is taken from the famous poem by Borges. The poems are grouped thematically, which is a method previously seen in the anthology of women poets by Marjorie Agosín. Each section of the book has a different title, such as "Dónde vivimos", "De dónde venimos", "El mundo que compartimos", "Lo que hacemos y adónde vamos", "Lo que somos y cómo amamos", and "Lo que será de nosotros"; in this rather Kantian classification, the content of each section is self-explanatory. The book includes the original poems as well as their translation into English, all of which allows us to appreciate both the original text in Castilian and the gargantuan work by Gwyn himself as an editor (which involved over ten years of travels and research) and translator.

Since we have mentioned the names of all poets included in previous anthologies (at the expense of the reader's patience!), in the case of the work by Gwyn it is more than justified to include all their names, especially as many of them are still writing and producing literary work today. Here they all are, classified according to their country of origin:

Colombia: Héctor Abad Faciolince, Piedad Bonett, Rómulo Bustos Aguirre, Alejandro Cortez González, Ramón Cote Baraibar, Carolina Dávila, Catalina González Restrepo, John Galán Casanova, Darío Jaramillo Agudelo, Juan Manuel Roca. **Guatemala:** Humberto Ak'Abal. **Uruguay:** Roberto Appratto, Rafael Courtoise, Eduardo Espina, Eduardo Milán. **Santo Domingo:** Frank Báez. **Chile:** Gustavo Barrera, Javier Bello, Camilo Brodsky, Carlos Decap, Damsi Figueroa, Marcelo Guajardo Thomas, Tomás Harris, Carlos Henrickson, Ricardo Herrera Alarcón, Jaime Huenún, Diego Maqueira, Jaime Pinos, Nadia Prado, Clemente Riedemann, Leonardo Sanhueza, Malí Urriola, Enrique Winter, Verónica Zondek, Raúl Zurita. **Venezuela:** Igor Barreto, Jaqueline Goldberg, Alicia Torres. **Nicaragua:** Gioconda Belli, Tania Montenegro. **Mexico:** Coral Bracho,

Antonio Deltoro, Jorge Fernández Granados, Luis Felipe Fabre, Ana Franco, Alicia García Begua, Julián Herbert, Claudia Hernández de Valle-Arispe, Carlos López Beltrán, Pura López Colomé, Tedi López Mills, Fabio Morabito, María Rivera, Pedro Serrano, Julio Trujillo. **Bolivia:** Mónica Velázquez Guzmán, Jessica Freudenthal Ovando, Gabriel Chávez Casasola. **Cuba:** Damaris Calderón, Wendy Guerra, Alessandra Molina. **Costa Rica:** Osvaldo Sauma, Paula Piedra, Luis Cháves. **Peru:** Micaela Chirif, Eduardo Chirinos, Miguel Ildefonso, Carmen Ollé. **Honduras:** Juan Ramón Saravia, Fabricio Estrada. **Ecuador:** Siomara España, Aleyda Quevedo Rojas. **El Salvador:** Osvaldo Hernández, Otoniel Guevara. **Argentina:** Teresa Arrijón, Jorge Aulicino, Diana Bellessi, Osvaldo Bossi, Fabián Casas, Alejandro Crotto, Edgar Dobry, Jorge Fonderbrider, Irene Gruss, Daniel Helder, Andrés Neuman, Miguel Petrecca, Sergio Raimondi, Mirta Rosenberg, Daniel Samoilovich, Marina Serrano, Ariel Williams, Laura Wittner. In terms of statistics, the book includes sixty-two men and thirty-five women; we are still a long way from equality.

Back to the beginning

Several poets included in the aforementioned anthologies lived in the United Kingdom at some point in their lives, as is the case with a number of contemporary poets. In fact, those in similar circumstances are aware that one of the more common drawbacks is the gradual loss of contact with literary circles that can assist with the dissemination and acknowledgement of their work both in their countries of origin and within the British literary and cultural environment, all of which is obviously the result of geographical and linguistic issues. In an attempt to redress this situation, at least partly, I set out to gather and compile the most relevant poetry efforts by Latin American writers who currently live and work in the UK, including myself. As I mentioned earlier, the initial goal was to make these poets known to the British public both in the original and in translation.

The emergence of **equidistancias** as a new publishing project was an unforeseen coincidence that we could not miss out on and a fitting chance to feature these writers; this was mainly because of its distinctiveness as a publisher aiming to showcase and divulge the work of Latin American poets also in the wider expanse from which they originated, which is Latin America.

As the project matured, other publishing initiatives took place in London.

One of such initiatives took place in 2017 under the publishing imprint Victorina Press founded by the indefatigable Consuelo Rivera-Fuentes. This was the bilingual book *Desentrañando memorias / Unravelling Memories*, the result of a literary award for poetry relating to historical memories and personal experiences linked to Latin American dictatorships. The book was translated by Guisela Parra-Molina and Reinaldo Ceballos. The first prize was awarded to poet Leonardo Boix (**Argentina**); the second prize, to Mabel Encinas (**Mexico**); and third prize, to María Eugenia Soto (**Peru**) and Gonzalo Núñez (**Chile**). Other writers who were shortlisted and later published included Paloma Zozaya (**Mexico**); Andreína Carrillo (**Venezuela**); Bárbara López Cardona (**Colombia**); Agustina Musante (**Argentina**); Isabel Rodas, Federico Sieder and Denisse Vargas-Bolaños (**Bolivia**); and Munir Eluti, Sara Galán Gil, Humberto Gatica-Leyton, Deni Lazo, Johnn Mendoza-Navarrete, Fermín Pávez, Enrique Quevedo, Valentina Montoya, Eliseo Vera and Juan Ramón Vergara (**Chile**).

Another initiative was the publication of an illustrated book to promote the Colombian group *Mujer Diáspora*, with poems by Nelly Mosquera, Sonia Quintero, Amparo Restrepo Vélez, Bárbara López Cardona, Angélica Quintero, Patricia Díaz, María Victoria Cristancho and Elizabeth Santander.

We must also mention the book *Todas las voces todas*, published by *El Ojo de la Cultura*, in 2019. This was an compilation of the poetry readings in Spanish "Leyendo Poesía In London", in which a number of Latin American poets took part (as well as authors from Spain and the UK): Sandra Dixon, Bárbara López Cardona, Fabián Álvarez, Jorge Naranjo, Jorge Paesano, Palmacera Suárez, Sonia Quinteros, Amparo Restrepo Vélez, Patricia Cardona and Juan Toledo (**Colombia**); Claudia Lozano (**Mexico**); Ana María Reyes (**Venezuela**); María Bravo-Calderara and Xaviera Ringeling (**Chile**); Isaac Suárez (**Dominican Republic**); and Enrique D. Zattara (**Argentina**).

Finally, there are several books and journals published by groups and organisations calling out to writers who are ethnically Latin American (most of them from English-speaking countries), though these poets generally write in English. Therefore, we have not considered them for this anthology, which is based solely on Spanish-speaking authors.

Why this selection of poets?

Compiling and editing an anthology can be a risky venture, mostly because it sometimes involves the immediate loss of friends. But difficulties also arise when compiling the work of writers who live and work away from their original environment and are usually outside local poetry circuits, particularly as they write in a language which is not the language of the country where they live. This is mostly the case with Latin American writers, as many of these creators (and typically the poets) are scattered, with few points of encounter to connect with others and establish contact. Accordingly, we would like to highlight the existence of various poetry collectives that group together Latin American writers in London; sometimes these collectives are short-lived and other times they work on a more permanent basis. To name but a few, publishers Victorina Press have taken a number of initiatives relating to publishing, events and literary awards; or independent publications like La Tundra; or the efforts of *Leyendo Poesía In London* (an initiative originally launched by the group "De lujurias y musas"), which organised a series of performance poetry events, with readings by at least fifty poets who write in Spanish and who are based in the UK.

Notwithstanding the possibility of insufficient information, accidental omissions or human error, we have embarked on this adventure despite all. I must add that we have most carefully scanned our field of enquiry and have carried out the relevant research with utmost rigour. As a result, we are convinced that all the poets in this anthology –and it will probably be missing a few names– most definitely deserve to be included.

I would like to discuss the criteria guiding our work.

Firstly, the poets in the anthology had to be of genuine Latin American origin (this means, born in Latin American countries where Castilian is spoken). This does not mean second or third generation Latin Americans, nor does it refer to family blood relationships or to Europeans who travelled abroad. It does mean poets born in Latin American countries and who are based *at present* in the UK.

Another condition was that the poems had to be written originally in Castilian. It is common and understandable that, at some point in their literary journey, the majority of poets who end up living and developing their creativity in the UK will try to write in English beyond translating their work. It is the case that we live and share our daily existence, both the personal and the literary, with communities whose first language is English, and it is certainly in our interest to be integrated into these communities and take part in the cultural landscape of this country. The result is that we almost always try to expand our poetic language into the mainstream language, and sometimes this is successfully achieved. However, for this anthology not only did we want to convey the individual creative makeup of the authors, but we aimed to specifically divulge their poetic production in the original language, in *our* language. This is why –although this may be considered debatable– we have not included poets originating from Brazil or from Caribbean nations, whether English or French-speaking. We must point out, however, that some of the poets in this anthology do include verses or stanzas in English or in *Spanglish* within their poems.

Above all else, we have strived to uphold the highest standards of quality in poetic expression. Of course, we do not consider ourselves indisputable judges in the field of aesthetic criteria, and even less in the context of poetry, which throughout its history has offered so many different manifestations in terms of creativity and experimentation. Indeed, there may be readers who do not agree with our selection criteria, and I am ready to accept this without any claim to infallibility. But I would like to emphasize that, whether I am right or wrong, my view is that the main requirement regarding "political poetry", "romantic poetry", "metaphysical poetry", "social poetry", "erotic poetry" or however you may wish to qualify poetry, is that it is **poetry**.

On the basis of these essential principles, there are other criteria that I consider important to highlight:

* Incorporating various aesthetic manifestations of poetic expression, and at the same time avoiding any type of discrimination or personal preferences.
* Achieving equitable representation of the various generations that constitute the Latin American community of poets in the UK.
* Drawing attention to any significant individual creative pathways resulting from their specific or historical importance in the context of creation and dissemination of poetry in Castilian within the UK.
* As the objective has been to deliver a sustained and consolidated poetic body of work, and not merely a collection of individual poems, we will aim to balance the quality and the trajectory of each of the poets, endeavouring to reconcile both criteria.

I would like to make it perfectly clear that I have not given in to any pressure whatsoever regarding what is politically correct as imposed by fashionable fads in discussion groups unrelated to Aesthetics itself, however immersed in the media they may be and whatever their noble-mindedness. When evaluating the poems in this anthology, no quotas were imposed and no positive discrimination was in force, nor were there any preconditions based on postcolonial ideas, gender, or any other considerations. The "progressive Victorian" ideals that permeate certain intellectual sectors are lately threatening with suffocating Art, lest it surrenders to considerations that are outside Art itself. This is most certainly not my approach. Neither have I considered achieving "national parity" among poets belonging to the various countries that make up the Latin American mosaic. The poets in the book are those who have been selected, and my purpose has been to underscore the quality of their poetry and not engage in discussions on geographical or any other type of representation.

Finally, I have always believed that one cannot get to know poets from solely one or two of their individual poems. Thus, we have preferred depth to assortment. This is the reason we have decided to include a smaller number of poets in order to be able to offer a wider perspective of their individual work.

Although the anthology is structured alphabetically, which is in itself a random classification, in this Introduction I would like to say a few words about the selected poets according to the generation to which they belong. The poets from the earlier generation are Chilean, as they are part of the considerable contingent of politically displaced migrants who arrived in London after the 1973 *coup d'état* by Augusto Pinochet in Chile. The collective of Chilean poets in London is one of the creative groups that has had the most exposure and longest track record. They left Chile at the beginning of the 1970's fleeing from the dictatorship of Pinochet, many of them having been imprisoned. For over half a century they have sustained strong links between them, as well as developing an intense literary activity, which in many cases meant endeavouring to write in English. It is within this Chilean collective that the 1988 book was published (mentioned at the beginning of this introduction, as well as the 2017 book also cited earlier), which positively inspired me to undertake this project. Among this collective of writers, Consuelo Rivera-Fuentes holds a prominent –extraordinarily prominent– place as the founder of the independent publisher Victorina Press. Consuelo is both a writer and an academic, and she has lived in the UK since 1992. The role that Victorina Press plays is indeed noteworthy because of the work it carries out to disseminate Latin American culture in the UK, mainly publishing Latin

American writers who live in this country. The literary countenance of this group of Chilean authors is strongly linked to their activism against the Pinochet dictatorship and with historical and collective memory, yet their writing expressly transcends these subjects, especially in the case of the poets, among which the most outstanding are **Eduardo Embry** and **María Eugenia Bravo Calderara**, whom we have chosen for this anthology. Both have published numerous works, particularly Eduardo Embry.

The next group is made up of authors who were born in the 1940's and 1950's and who came to live in London; their experiences as immigrants were different and distinctive. Some of them belonged to the academic world, as is the case of **Alberto Paucar Cáceres** and **Luis Rebaza Soraluz**, both from Peru, and **Diego de Jesús Flores-Jaime** from Mexico. Others have been in the UK for over half a century, arriving here when emigrating to the UK was an adventure not many opted for; this is the case of **Carlos Sapochnik**, who began to publish his invaluable and hitherto unknown poetry only in the last decade. The Colombian **Juan Toledo** has led a nomadic life, and before settling in London he lived in the US and in Madrid; although renowned as one of the major cultural activists in Latin American circles in the UK, he has kept his own poetry in the dark until the publication of his first and only book so far. In my case, I am one of the more recent arrivals in London, having published initially in Buenos Aires and then in Spain (where I lived for a quarter of a century) seven poetry collections between 1978 and 2020.

The following generation includes **Óscar Guardiola-Rivera**. He is one of the most distinguished Latin American cultural figures in the UK as a result of his activism and his political writing, and has a notable presence in the world of poetry. **Juana Aldock** is a prominent Mexican poet who lives in Glasgow. **Leonardo Boix**, from Argentina, is the recipient of several awards for poetry in Castilian and English, and has promoted several initiatives in tutoring and dissemination of literature of ethnic Latin American origin, some of them jointly with another prominent cultural manager, Nathalie Teitler. This is also the case of the Colombian **Sebastián Montes**, whose writing is only known is small writing circles.

Finally, there is a group of younger writers who have recently arrived in this, their British destiny, and who are still in a stage of training and learning, as well as taking part regularly in the many poetry readings and performance poetry events that flourish in London. Many of them, as I said previously in this introduction, have decided to take English on board in order to facilitate their integration into the local cultural environment, but this does not mean that they have given up writing poetry in Castilian. We look forward to their continuing development as poets; some of them are included in this anthology because they have reached, at least in my view, a level of excellence in their writing that makes them worthy of being featured. This is the case of **Xaviera Ringeling** (Chile), who has published a single book of poetry until now; **Ana María Reyes Barrios** (Venezuela); **Gaby Sambucetti** (Argentina); and **Lester Gómez Medina** (Nicaragua-Costa Rica).

During my research, I have tried to reach out to as many poetry groups as feasible, but undoubtedly it is impossible to encompass them all. I believe, unwittingly yet unerringly, that there will be those who claim, whether in all justice or not, that certain indispensable voices are missing from this anthology. If this is the case, I profusely apologise beforehand, but readers of the book will likely empathise with the enormous difficulties of the task that we have undertaken.

I believe this anthology effectively epitomises the publishing criteria identifying our imprint *Equidistancias*. This is why we have chosen the title *Voces equidistantes* for the book. Thus, if one of the previously published anthologies we mentioned earlier was conceited enough – inadvertently, I presume– to be called *Antología **de los** poetas latinoamericanos*, this volume will have the much less pretentious title of *Antología **de** poetas latinoamericanos…*

And what remains now is for you to read and delight in the poems by the following selection of poets. I hope you enjoy their work as much as I enjoyed the groundwork, research and editing of the book.

ENRIQUE D. ZATTARA
Director, El Ojo de la Cultura Hispanoamericana
London, March 2023

Introduction to the translation of this book

Translating 'Voces Equidistantes' into English and transforming the text into 'Equidistant Voices' has been as intense as it was fascinating and as challenging as it was rewarding. I am grateful to have worked with such exquisite poems, ideas, and images, and to have been given the chance to honour the exceptional poets included in this unique anthology.

The translation of poetry is not so much a linguistic undertaking as a literary one. In the case of this book, the translated poems were submitted to each individual poet for comments, and their suggestions were mostly incorporated into the final version. With translation being the complex and dynamic discipline that it is, it would have been ideal to engage in further debate, especially as poetry is largely susceptible to multiple interpretations –after all, it is an art form that suggests more than it says– but we had a strict timeline to adhere to. In all, 'Equidistant Voices' is the result of the fruitful collaboration between the editor, the translator and the poets themselves.

The translated version of the book is, I trust, a collection of poems that can be read in English with the same ease as in the original Castilian, with both the poetic and the existential spilling over into the target text. I have tried to keep to the flow and musicality of words and expressions, using the colloquial or the lyrical as required and delving into hidden messages and metalinguistic elements in an attempt to convey first and emulate later. From a more technical stance, I have followed similar punctuation (or should I say, lack of it), which is sometimes a difficult read in the original but can be heavenly from a rhythmic point of view; however, I have occasionally included additional punctuation in the translated text, certainly not to disrupt the flow but to ensure that images are well defined and concepts are grasped. I have endeavoured to find equivalences regarding alliteration and pace in the target language, and I have customised some of the imagery.

For the purposes of clarity, I have very occasionally added in English what was not verbalised explicitly in the original text yet was very much there.

In essence, the translated texts are poems of poems, inspired and enthused by the original texts, which will be interpreted anew with each reading. This is my version of the collected poems in the book, in the same way that readers will develop their own version, whether in English or in Castilian. As linguists we must be true to the original, but as poets our mission is to write poetry. Ultimately, the translation of poetry is a journey, as exhilarating and arduous as the poet's journey.

Isabel del Rio
Poet, Fiction-Writer and Linguist

Isabel del Rio is a British-Spanish writer and linguist. Born in Madrid, she has lived in London most of her life. She has a five-year *Licenciatura* (Universidad Complutense) and is a Fellow of both the Chartered Institute of Linguists (CIoL) and the Institute of Translation and Interpreting (ITI); she is currently studying for a PhD in Creative Writing, with Translation and Adaptation as her main subjects of study. She has worked as a full-time broadcaster, journalist and translator for the BBC World Service, and for over two decades as a full-time translator and terminologist for a London-based United Nations agency. Being a bilingual author, she has published fiction and poetry in both English and Spanish, including *La duda* (shortlisted for two literary awards), *Paradise & Hell*, and *A Woman Alone: fragments of a memoir*; her poetry includes *Madrid Madrid Madrid*, *Dolorem Ipsum*, and *Cuaderno de notas*. Her most recent book is *La autora del fin del mundo*, published by **equidistancias**; it is an anthology of her short stories from the past three decades and which includes both stories originally written in Spanish and her translated versions of stories originally written in English. As a language practitioner, Isabel has extensive experience in literary, documentary, institutional, and technical translation, and she is also involved in tutoring, mentoring and lecturing in translation and creative writing. She is the co-founder of the independent imprint Friends of Alice Publishing (FoA) and her website is *www.isabeldelrio.co.uk*

Equidistant voices
Voces equidistantes

JUANA ADCOCK
(Mexico)

Juana Adcock was born in Monterrey, Mexico, in 1982, and she has lived in Glasgow since 2009. She has translated the work of Diego Osorno, Gabriela Wiener, Julia Navarro and Giuseppe Caputo, among others. Her first poetry collection *Manca* was published in 2014; the Mexican critic Sergio González Rodríguez stated that it was the best book published that year. Her work has appeared in magazines such as *Words Without Borders*, *Asymptote*, and *Glasgow Review of Books*.

Juana Adcock nació en Monterrey, México en 1982, y actualmente reside en Glasgow (Escocia) desde 2009. Como traductora, ha trabajado la obra de Diego Osorno, Gabriela Wiener, Julia Navarro o Giuseppe Caputo entre otros. Su primera colección de poemas, Manca *(2014), fue calificada por el crítico mexicano Sergio González Rodríguez como el mejor libro de poesía del año. Su obra ha sido publicada en revistas como* Words Without Borders, Asymptote, *and* Glasgow Review of Books.

Note by the Translator: some of Juana's poems are written using both English and Spanish. The Spanish sections in these particular poems have been translated into English and appear in *italics*.

Puertas que abiertas hacia adentro arden

Qué bendita dicha la de poder cerrar los ojos y ver
alguien cerrar los ojos

Que su antebrazo sienta las gotas y casi
antes de preguntar qué pasa se desmenuce su
garganta en el suelo

Y qué bendita llave la que abría todas las puertas,
la que
una tela humilde cruzábanos sus nudillos como
manos en rezo
unos nudos temblorosos que se trenzaban en fardos, unos talones
¿quieres desnudar todos mis nudos? ¿abrir todas mis puertas?
        sí, quiero abrir las puertas en tu pie: beso, las puertas en la uña de tu dedo gordo:
beso, las puertas en tu astrágalo: beso, las puertas en tu sóleo: beso, las puertas en tu
sartorio: beso, las puertas en tu pectíneo: beso, las puertas en tu hipocondrio: las puertas
en tu aspecto ventral: beso, las puertas en tu occipital: beso, las puertas en tu foramen
mago:
beso, las puertas en tu hallucis brevis: beso, las
puertas en tu vago: beso, las puertas en tu subclavia: beso, las puertas en tu proceso
transverso: beso, las puertas en tu región del vacío, etcétera

Ayer vi los párpados volando hechos pedazos
los sitios salobres donde nos andábamos llorando
los huecos desanclados, desarraigados
el delgado canto que en la mañana nos alzaba

esa madre que no tengo, el huevo
detrás de mi cuello donde el hueco es el huevo es el hueco donde se gesta
el principio donde nace, esa sangre que se espesa, que se dispersa, que nos amarra

Doors that burn when opening inwards

What blessed joy when you close your eyes and see
someone else closing their eyes

and their forearm feeling the drops falling on it and, before they have
time to ask what the matter is, their throat crumbles and falls to pieces on
the floor

And the blessed key that can open all doors,
the humble weave crossing knuckles like
praying hands,
trembling knots braided as bundles,
or heels
Is it that you wish to bare all my knots? Or open
all my doors?
         yes, I want to open the door on your foot: I kiss, the doors
on the nail of your big toe: I kiss, doors on your
talus; I kiss, doors on your soleus; I kiss, doors
on your sartorius: I kiss, doors
on your pectineus; I kiss, doors
on your hypochondrium; doors
on your ventral aspect: I kiss, doors
on your occipital: I kiss, doors
on your foramen magnum: I kiss
doors on your hallucis brevis: I kiss, doors on
your vagus: I kiss, doors on your subclavian:
I kiss, doors on your transverse process: I kiss, doors
on your void region, etcetera

Yesterday I saw flying eyelids torn to bits
the brackish places where we would cry

La neta: este piquete de avispa es mi única
pertenencia, esa agua que se hacina detrás
de las puertas en mi cara

Taquitos de frijoles

Voy a hacer unos taquitos de frijoles,
para que se desayunen antes de ir a trabajar.
La estufa hechiza. La olla de aluminio golpeado.
Dejo los frijoles a fuego lento, lentísimo,
y me voy a dormir porque no puedo más.
Es de madrugada ya, y entre sueños,
siento la llama apagarse, la casa llena de gas.
¿Te acuerdas cómo abrimos el ojo
sin poder mover ni la cara,
y con el miedo de que una chispa mínima?
Pero en realidad desperté ya muy tarde,
la olla negra, los frijoles ceniza, el fuego
todavía diligente.
Mi marido sigue soñando los tacos de su madre.
Y yo, no incendié la casa ni nos maté asfixiados.
Me dicen mis hijos: ¿traemos de lata, aunque sepan a lata, mamá?

the anchorless hollow spaces, unrooted
the tenuous song that would hoist us in the morning

the mother I do not have, the egg
behind my neck where the hollow is the egg is the
hollow gestating the commencement where it is born, the
blood that thickens and disperses, mooring us

The absolute truth: this bee sting is my only
belonging, water
piling up behind the doors on my face

Little bean tacos

I'm going to prepare some little bean tacos
for your breakfast before you set off for work.
The stove casts a spell. A hammered aluminium pan.
I leave the beans to cook on a low heat, so very low,
and then I go to sleep because I cannot take it anymore.
It is early morning and, in my dreams, I feel
the flame extinguishing, the house filling with gas fumes.
Do you remember how we opened our eyes
without being able to move even our face,
afraid as we were of the slightest spark?

But what happened was that I woke up so very late,
the pan was blackened, the beans were ash, the
fire was still working hard.
My husband still dreams of his mother's tacos.

Una casa dentro de otra casa

Sabía tocarle la nuca
doblarla de parte a parte
haciendo un origami de su espíritu
pusilánime.
Cada doblez, pared con
pared, techo y columna.
Abrir las ventanas y que
entre la lluvia.

*

Una casa con sus larguísimas piernas
hacía genuflexión sobre la arena.
Su cuerpo era una nave y él marinero
mareándose en la tierra.

*

En el cuerpo se escondía ella: una casa
dentro de otra casa
dentro de otra casa
para que no pudiera tocarla.

And on my part, I didn't burn the house down nor did I kill everyone
at home by choking them to death.
And children ask me this: shall we get a tin, mum, even though they
will have a tinny taste?

A house within a house

She knew how to touch his nape
folding it from one end to the other
making an origami cut-out from his
feeble spirit.

Each fold, wall with wall,
ceiling and column
Open the windows, may
the rain come in.

*

A house with its exceedingly long legs
would genuflect on the sand
Her body was a vessel and he was a sailor
who would pass out on land.

*

She would hide in that body: a house
within a house
within a house
so that no one could touch her.

Dónde comprar pan

Tener doce años justo antes de la hora de comer
a mediodía con el pavimento tendido al sol
y que te manden a la tienda de la esquina a comprar pan.
Salir por la puerta
sin haber jamás menstruado
vestida en jeans camiseta y tenis
plegable como una espiga verde de trigo
que agita su cabeza en el viento

poner un pie delante del otro
sentir la comezón
del brassiere
blanco sin alambres
talla 28A
manos en los bolsillos, sol en la corona.

Buscar la propia sombra bajo los pies y pensar en una canción
al escuchar un silbido desde la cima
del edificio a medio construir y la palabra
mamasita.
No mirar hacia arriba ni ver las estructuras de cemento desnudo o los fierros rojo-óxido
salidos.

Seguir caminando y decirte a ti misma
que eres fuerte.

Where can you buy bread

Being twelve years old just before lunchtime
with the pavement laid out under the sun at midday
on an errand to the corner shop to buy a loaf of bread.
Going out through the door without
ever having menstruated
dressed in your jeans, t-shirt, sneakers,
you are as supple as a green ear of wheat
shaking its head in the wind, and so you
place one foot in front of the other
feeling the itchiness brought on by your
brassiere,
it's a white one with no underwire,
size 28A;
hands in your pockets, sun on top of your head.

Looking for a shadow under your feet, you think
about a song
instead of the wolf-whistling coming from high above
the half-built structure as well as the word
mamasita, you little hot momma, you!
And yet not looking upwards nor seeing the bare cement structures nor
all those protruding metal segments in oxide-red.

So, you go on walking and say to yourself:
"You're strong!"

Tengo una idea para una novela

Tengo una idea para una novela.
El méthodo será simple:
jigsaw spaces que se desbaratan and interchange

baldíos for billboards
shop speak por solecismos y un río stopping short
abandoned high street windows for maniquís rotos,
cáscara de naranja, industrial machinery, éxitos de todos los tiempos, puntas de flecha,
canned sardines, bultos de cemento, community halls, a baby's shoe.

Las memorias de un gran emprendedor
escritas en las piedras, castillos, fundidoras, diócesis.
Un tren dividing the meadows, a grating touch
of airport peinando zurcos in the air.

Una sultana ladera de la montaña
donde tallaron los huecos de las moradas y los locales de triciclos
la ciudad entera in fact, in those cavities
          (scrawny ladders joining one street to the next)
que en la noche brilla como árbol navideño.

Y en este tumulto encontraré lugar para el pathos,
repeating elements, la illusion of unity y una resolución tan espectacular
it will soften the eye:

un ojo de agua, a word
made into flesh

I have an idea for a novel

I have an idea for a novel.
I will follow a simple method:
jigsaw spaces *that are thrown into disarray* and interchange

wastelands for billboards
shop speak for *solecisms and a river* stopping short
abandoned high street windows for *broken mannequins,*
orange peel, industrial machinery, *successes*
achieved over time, arrowheads, canned
sardines, *bags of cement*, community halls, a baby's shoe.

The memories of a great entrepreneur
written in stone, castles, foundries, dioceses.
A train dividing the meadows, a grating touch
of airport *combing gullies* in the air.

A slope on the mountain
as beautiful as the wife of a sultan
where they carved out the opening of dwellings and the sites
for tricycles
the whole town in fact, in those cavities
          (scrawny ladders joining one street to the next)
that shine at night like a Christmas tree.

And it that turmoil I will find a place for pathos,
repeating elements, *the* illusion of unity *and such*
a spectacular steadfastness that it will soften the eye:

an eye made out of water, a word
made into flesh.

Tres seasons

1. I know how she does it:

"¡Look at how I stand
out from the crowd!
My unique uniqueness un resplandor
around my crown"

She makes the most of every piece,
wastes not one.
She seams together the debris
to beautiful, coherent whole

She creates, creaks open the door
into which a trap, a trip
across the mushy fields;
a place can only take her so far

Trip white Fergus, silent Fergus,
snow on Kelvingrove.
La línea negra de sus párpados
rasguea sus ojos a la chinoise

Y donde los árboles hicieron su lento striptease
revelando una cumbre horizontal de luces
the light recedes over the white hills
the rain punctures the snow, dalmationing

Y el hiato entre mis cariadas muelas
dice let me say, without irony:
dip your fingers in the clay

Three seasons

1. I know how she does it:

"Look at how I stand
out from the crowd!
My unique uniqueness *a radiance*
around my crown"

She makes the most of every piece,
wastes not one.
She seams together the debris
to beautiful, coherent whole

She creates, creaks open the door
into which a trap, a trip
across the mushy fields;
a place can only take her so far

Trip white Fergus, silent Fergus,
snow on Kelvingrove.
The black line on her eyelids
scrawling her eyes a la chinoise

And where trees performed their slow striptease
revealing a horizontal summit of luminance
the light recedes over the white hills
the rain punctures the snow, dalmationing

And the hiatus between my decayed molars
declares let me say, without irony:
dip your fingers in the clay

in the early days we had only ourselves.

2. Ella tiene diamantes incrustados en los lagrimales.

Por eso la quieren más que a mí.
Por eso y por los rayos verdes de su photocopy machine.
(And for saying yes cuando digo no
not really, to be on my own)

Ella tiene, como iba diciendo, la boca
llena de murciélagos.
Cuando sonríe las alas se extienden,
acarician dientes.

Por eso la quieren más que a mí.
Sus ojos, por otro lado,
de verde-cielo se van haciendo cafés
con las hojas en otoño.

Era halloween, por ejemplo, when the bats
leapt out of her mouth.
She almost died in her sleep.
I was still green.

3. Her hair is a forest in flames.

Yesterday, if i remember well
la post office was a parranda where all parcels were opened.
I armed myself against her beauty.
I laughed out loud.

in the early days we had only ourselves.

2. *Diamonds incrusted in her tear glands.*

That is why they love her more than they love me.
Because of that, and because of the green rays in her photocopy machine.
(And for saying yes *when I say* no
not really, to be on my own)

As I was saying, her mouth
is full of bats.
And when she smiles, their wings expand
caressing her teeth.

That is why they love her more than they love me.
Her eyes, on the other hand,
of a green-skyblue colour depart making coffee
with Autum leaves.

It was halloween, for example, when the bats
leapt out of her mouth.
She almost died in her sleep.
I was still green.

3. Her hair is a forest in flames.

Yesterday, if I remember well
the post office was a *rave* where all parcels were opened.
I armed myself against her beauty.
I laughed out loud.

Todos los días I imagine
cómo sería being married to you
financial hardship, porque siempre hay deudas, hipotecas
lips, naked shoulders
next day amanecemos
tú poniéndote los zapatos
yo haciendo café
tendríamos cats for kids
books for lovers y huajes to drink
I was never much for linen
pero lo era en el fondo.
Es el slag
del tiempo
I was to live
         under.
I don't sé
qué me da más miedo:
conventions routine
falling head first,
all that I no pude,
giving up what hurts.
I've been despidiéndome of you
desde before we met
que entraste into the room
wearing my skirt
and I knew
que you no eras all para tenerte
and I would both be going siempre lejos away.

Every single day I imagine
how it would feel being married to you
financial hardship, *because there are always debts,*
mortgages
lips, naked shoulders
next day *we would wake up*
you putting on your shoes
and me making coffee
we would have cats for kids
books for lovers *and gourds* to drink
I was never much for linen
but then deep down I was.
It is the slag
of time
I was to live
         under.
I don't *know*
what frightens me most:
conventions routine
falling head first,
all that I *could not,*
giving up what hurts.
I've been saying *goodbye to you*
since before we met
and you came into the room
wearing my skirt
and I knew
that you *were not* all *to be had*
and I would both be going *always far* away.

LEONARDO BOIX
(Argentina)

Leo Boix was born in Argentina and lives in the UK. His two poetry collections in Spanish, *Un Lugar Propio* (2015) and *Mar de Noche* (2017), were published by Letras del Sur Editora. He has also published a poetry collection in English *Ballad of a Happy Immigrant* (Penguin/Random House, 2021); which was awarded the Poetry Book Society Wild Card Choice. His work has been included in many anthologies, among them *Ten Poets of the New Generation* (Bloodaxe), *The Best New British and Irish Poets Anthology 2019-2020* (Eyewear Publishing) and *Un Nuevo Sol: British Latinx Writers* (flipped eye). His poetry has been published in many British and international publications. He is the recipient of several awards, including the Bart Wolffe Poetry Prize (2018) and the Keats-Shelley Prize (2019).

Leo Boix nació en Argentina y vive en el Reino Unido. Ha publicado dos libros de poesía en español Un Lugar Propio, *2015, y* Mar de Noche, *2017, ambos con Letras del Sur Editora, además de un poemario en inglés* Ballad of a Happy Immigrant *(Penguin/Random House, 2021), que obtuvo un galardón especial del Poetry Book Society de Londres. Ha sido incluido en muchas antologías, entre ellas* Ten Poets of the New Generation *(Bloodaxe),* The Best New British and Irish Poets Anthology *2019-2020 (Eyewear Publishing) y* Un Nuevo Sol: British Latinx Writers *(flipped eye). Sus poemas han sido publicados en numerosas revistas británicas e internacionales. Ha obtenido varios premios, incluidos el Bart Wolffe Poetry Prize 2018 y el Keats-Shelley Prize 2019.*

El juicio final (1482)
Basado en 'El Juicio Final", de Jerónimo El Bosco

No es fácil entrar a la casa del infierno
hay que pedir permiso, un monstruo

encendido te hace pasar. El búho
protege la entrada. Los sapos decoran

la puerta del más allá. No grites, esperá:
El cardenal de rojo leerá tu testamento,

habrá mitad-animales. Tus pecados
vendados, una espada te atravesará el pecho.

Tu segunda esposa llamó al cura para la unción.
Yo trago el monólogo in extremis detrás del sofá.

Sueños del demonio para el último baile.
Y canta: El juicio final está llegando.

Se mueve en un círculo perfecto, en sincronía.
Y canta: Ten piedad de nosotros.

Completa el tríptico. El hombre verde
devora la carne, mira al paraíso.

Una flecha cruza su cabeza.
Parece muerto, la boca, los ojos semi abiertos.

Aún le sale fuego de adentro.
Una pincelada simple amarillo, rojo, magenta.

The Final Judgment (1482)
Based on The Final Judgment by Hieronymus Bosch

No, it is not easy to enter the House of Hell,
you must first ask for permission, a monster

on fire will allow you entry. An owl protects
the entrance. Toads embellish

the door leading to the afterlife. Don't shout but wait:
that cardinal robed in red will deliver your will,

there shall be creatures, half-human and half-beast. Your sins
bound with bandages, a sword shall pierce your chest.

Your second wife called out to the cleric for the anointing.
From behind the sofa, I guzzle that solo speech at death's door.

They are but the devil's dreams meant for one last dance.
And thus, he chants: The Final Judgement is coming.

Moving within a perfect circle, it is all synchronised.
And thus, he chants again: Have mercy on us.

This completes the tryptic. The green man
devours flesh whilst looking at Paradise.

An arrow punctures his head. He looks as if he is dead,
you can tell from both his mouth and his half-closed eyes.

Fire still gushes from him.
They're but basic brushstrokes in yellow, red, magenta.

San Jerónimo (1490-1500)

Rezaba como vos, a lo muerto
¿pero a quién? ¿para qué?
        su cama, una piedra simple
imperfecta. Bajala un poco, hijo
                hacé que se vaya el dolor. Un ruego,
paisaje expandiéndose en tonos verdes.

        Como la suya, tu capa roja abandonada,
un sombrero de paja en la orilla del río Lete. Vos—
reflejo
que nunca volvió.

Rezaste incrédulo.
        Tu perro no quería abandonarte, lamió
tus suturas secas. Más flaco—
rama retorcida del árbol que nunca plantamos.

Sin ceremonias,
    el viento se detuvo.

        En el estanque cercano,
la piel de un fruto seco naufragaba,
un pato de plástico
                        presentía tu muerte.

De una isla con un puente caído,
reapareció un pequeño pájaro muerto. Tal vez león—
compañero del santo, leo *te miraba*
desde la orilla.
Felino dócil, como flor de campo, fuera de lugar.

Saint Jerome (1490-1500)

Like you, he prayed for the dead
but to whom and what for?
    his bed, a simple and imperfect
stone. *Lower it a little, my son,*
        make the pain go away. A plea,
an expanding landscape in green hues.

    Like his, your red cape is cast off,
a straw-hat on the banks of the river Lethe. It is you—
a reflection
that never once returned.

You prayed yet were unbelieving.
    Your dog did not want to leave your side, licking
as he did your dried sutures. So skinny—
a warped branch of the tree we would never plant.

The wind ceased to blow
    without making a fuss,

    In the nearby pond,
the husk from a nut foundered,
a plastic duck
        foretold your death.

From an island with a collapsed bridge, there
reappeared a small dead bird. Perhaps a lion
–the saint's companion, *leo* watched you
from the riverbank.
Such a docile feline, just like a wildflower, was out of place.

Bajá la cama, hijo, más todavía,
        hacé que se vaya el dolor.

Pájaros, -tus favoritos-, cantaron en el funeral.
        Acostado, boca abajo
sobre la tierra, enriqueciendo el humus del limonero.

Más allá de las rocas, un río serpenteando, una iglesia en desuso,
una granja que visitaste antes que naciera.
Desde una rama alta
el venteveo te llamaba.
Más tarde el fuego lo devoró todo.

Cuando vino el cura, le contaste tus miedos.
Nosotros dejamos la habitación, insectos
escapando a sus escondites,

y nunca más regresamos.

Cómo embalsamar un cuerpo
Basado en 'La muerte y el avaro' (1494) de Jerónimo El Bosco

I

                [Desvestir el cuerpo, dejarlo sobre la mesa de embalsamamiento]

Fue llevado por una mariposa blanca y negra con cabeza de ratón,
una rana cubría su pequeño pene, por debajo le brotaba sangre.
Sus manos estaban atadas por la espalda. Tenía manchas púrpuras en la cara.

Lower the bed, my child, lower it more,
        make the pain go away.

Birds –your favourite birds– sang at your funeral.
        Reclining, face down
on the earth, enriching the humus of the lemon-tree.

Beyond the rocks, a winding river, a
deserted church,
a farm you visited before my birth.
From a high branch
the great kiskadee called out to you.
But then fire devoured it all.

And when the priest arrived, you told him about your fears.
As we left the room, insects
ran to their hiding places,

and we never returned.

How to embalm a body
Based on 'Death and the Miser' (1494) by Hieronymus Bosch

I

                        [Undress the body and place it on the embalming table]

He was taken away by a black and white butterfly bearing
The head of a mouse,
a frog covered its little penis, and under it

Le escuché decir algo antes de jadear. ¿Un nombre?
¿Un lugar en el que estuvimos juntos alguna vez?

II

[Afeitar el rostro, limpiar las expresiones faciales. Llenar la cavidad oral, los ojos
con algodón, las zonas hundidas de la cara, balancear la nariz para lograr una apariencia
facial placentera antes de iniciar el proceso de embalsamamiento]

Beso hueco. Sien hundida. Manos vacías.
Un pájaro encaramado en la medianera lo mira.

Parece dormido. Sueña con pequeños insectos:
avispas, abejas, gorgojos en limones. Muy cerca,

una salamandra moteada con un sombrero rojo
cuenta las hojas caídas de un duraznero. Le faltan
dos ojos. Después de muerto, su cara se volvió repugnante.

III

[Levantar la carótida o la arteria braquial. Cortar el cuerpo, buscando la arteria
para inyectarle formol. Dependiendo del caso o preferencia del embalsamador, cualquiera
de estas arterias puede ser utilizada para inyectarse el fluido embalsamador].

blood was flowing.
His hands were tied behind his back. He had purple stains on his face.
I heard him say something before he began to gasp. A name?
A place where we were together once?

II

[Shave the face, clean the facial features. Before starting the embalming process, fill the oral cavity and eyes with cotton wool as well as the sunken areas in the face, poise the nose to attain a pleasant facial expression]

A hollow kiss. A collapsed temple. Empty hands.
A bird perched on the dividing wall stares at him.

It looks as if he is asleep. He dreams of small insects:
wasps, bees, weevils inside lemons. So close,

a speckled salamander with a red hat
counts the leaves that have fallen from a peach-tree. He is missing
his two eyes. Once dead, his face became repugnant.

III

[Lift either the carotid artery or the brachial artery. Make an incision to get to the artery and inject formaldehyde. Depending on each case, or on the embalmer's preferences, any of these two arteries can be used to inject the embalming fluid].

Estaba dolorido, nadie lo notaba.
Con los días sus piernas cada vez más flacas.
Huesos como astas de ciervo arropadas en ángulo.

No había superficies suaves, sólo manchas, pequeños caminos
sobre la piel, lagos estancados. Quería que lo llevaran
a una torre circular. Pero no podía decirlo.

Su voz de hielo
La salamandra sugirió un nicho arriba, en el 4to piso.

IV

*[Inyectar el fluido embalsamador en la arteria, drenar las venas yugular, femoral
o braquial, utilizando una máquina embalsamadora. Esta máquina inyecta formol en el
cuerpo, mientras fuerza la salida de sangre].*

Para cuando me fui a él le quedaba muy poco. Sus dedos
no se movían como debían. Una última caricia.

Gotas de sangre seca en sus uñas.
¿Nos escuchás hablando de vos?

Un suspiro, otro jadeo. La radio aún prendida:
Olinda Bozán cantando 'Saludó y se fue'.

He was sore and aching, but no one noticed.
As days went by, his legs became thinner.
His bones were like antlers tucked in angles.

There were no soft surfaces, only blemishes, tiny paths
along the skin, stagnant lakes. He wished to be taken
to a circular tower. But he could not bring himself to say it.

With its icy voice
the salamander suggested a higher niche in the cemetery, the one on the fourth level.

IV

[Inject the embalming fluid into the artery, drain the jugular, femoral or brachial veins by means of an embalming machine, which injects formaldehyde into the body, whilst pushing out the blood].

By the time I went away, he had little time left. His fingers
did not move as they should. A final caress.

Drops of dried blood on his nails.
Can you hear us talking about you?

A sigh, a gasp. The radio is still on:
Olinda Bozán is signing 'He greeted us and left'.

V

[Punzar, aspirar todos los órganos principales del torso utilizando una aguja trocar recta o curva para perforar la pared del tórax, conectada a un hidro-aspirador. Luego, la cavidad se rellena con una solución altamente concentrada de formol].

Dentro de la habitación todo era calma. Ninguna luz
podía entrar desde el living. Llovió. Paró.
Volvió a llover. El diario del domingo doblado cuidadosamente.

Una almohada para la enfermera. Tu andador,
criatura prehistórica ya sin uso.
Un platito con comida que no podías tragar.

Cajas apiladas de medicamentos de todos colores.
Tu pañuelo escondido debajo de las sábanas manchadas.
¿Escuchás la lluvia inundando el patio de atrás?

Una voz baja burbujeando
junto al tanque de oxígeno,
agua destilada para humedecer la última frase.

VI

[Lavar bien el cuerpo. Usar un jabón especial germicida para desinfectar el cuerpo embalsamado].

Era demasiado tarde para las uvas,
sin embargo vinieron los mirlos, uno por uno.

V

[With a trocar needle, whether straight or curved and connected to a hydro aspirator, perforate the thoracic wall, and all main organs contained in the trunk will be punctured and aspirated. After this has been completed, the cavity shall then be filled with a solution that includes a high concentration of formaldehyde].

Inside the room it was calm. No light
coming from the living room. It rained. It stopped raining.
It rained again. The Sunday paper was carefully folded.

There was a pillow for the nurse. Your walker was
now a prehistoric creature without a purpose.
A small plate with food you could no longer swallow.

Piles of boxes with multicoloured medication.
Your handkerchief hidden under the stained sheets.
Can you hear the rain flooding the backyard?

A voice bubbling up
alongside the oxygen tank,
distilled water to moisten the last phrase.

VI

[Wash the body thoroughly. Use a special germicide soap to disinfect the embalmed body].

It was too late for grapes,
yet the blackbirds arrived, one by one.

Se fue juntando polvo debajo de tu sillón favorito.
Yo me iba ese día, vos lo sabías de memoria.

Te prometí que plantaría un limonero en tu honor.

VII

[Sellar las incisiones con costura, aplicar líquido adhesivo en la zona. Una vez que el cuerpo queda sellado, las incisiones deben ser cubiertas con plástico para evitar derrames].

Como estatuas tomadas de la mano,
un secreto al mediodía, los labios se sellaron.

Las células comenzaron a descomponerse rápido
a medida que el corazón se detenía.

El tuyo no. En la cocina
esperaron que me fuera.

Yo no podía levantar mis valijas.

The dust collected under your favourite armchair.
I would leave that day, and you knew this by heart.

I promised that I would plant a lemon-tree in your memory.

VII

[Seal the incisions with sutures and apply adhesive liquid to the area. Once
the body is sealed, the incisions must be covered
with plastic to avoid leakage].

Like statues holding hands,
lips were sealed, a midday secret.

Cells began to quickly decompose
as the heart was coming to a halt.

But not yours. In the kitchen
they were waiting for me to leave.

I could not lift my suitcases.

VIII

[Vestir al cuerpo, prepararlo para su exposición].

Una voz entrecortada: 'Como quien va
Para no volver, me miró al pasar
Saludó y se fue. ¡No lo he visto más!'.

Todo ocurrió a las 18.20. Los árboles al costado
de la pista de despegue se volvieron ocre, colorados.

Sicómoros. Eucalipto de las pampas.
Su vuelo ascendía. La enfermera corría para dar la noticia.

'Como quien va, Para no volver,
Me miró al pasar, saludó y se fue. ¡No lo he visto más!'

VIII

[Dress the body and prepare it for display].

A faltering voice: 'Like someone who leaves
to never return, he looked at me as he passed by, greeted me
and left. No, I never saw him again!'.

It all happened at 18.20. The trees alongside
the take-off runway turned ochre, ruddy.

Sycamores. Eucalyptus tree of the pampa.
The flight ascended. The nurse ran to give everyone the news.

'Like someone who leaves
to never return, he looked at me as he passed by, greeted me
and left. No, I never saw him again!'

MARÍA BRAVO-CALDERARA
(Chile)

María Eugenia Bravo-Calderara is a poet, fiction writer, ex-political prisoner during the Chilean dictatorship, and an exile in the UK. Her writing has been published in all European languages, as well as Finnish, Arabic and Tamil. She is the author of several poetry collections *Oración en el Estadio Nacional* and *Poems from Exile*. Her memoir *La Casa del Techo Rojo*, is soon to be published in Chile. She belongs to the *Taller de Literatura de la Memoria de las mujeres hispanoamericanas de Londres*. The poetry she wrote when she was a political prisoner is permanently on display on the walls of the museums of memory in Chile.

María Eugenia Bravo-Calderara es poeta, narradora, exprisionera política de la dictadura chilena, exiliada en Inglaterra. Sus escritos han sido publicados en todas las lenguas europeas además del finés, el árabe y el tamil. Es autora de los poemarios Oración en el Estadio Nacional, *y* Poems from Exile. *La Casa del Techo Rojo, memorias, está por aparecer pronto en Chile. Es miembro del Taller de Literatura de la Memoria de las mujeres hispanoamericanas de Londres. En Chile la poesía que compuso siendo prisionera política hoy día está en exhibición permanente en los muros de los museos de la memoria.*

Perdonadme

Perdonadme estos dolores que recuento
y que repito.

Perdonadme estos cortejos funerarios,
esta cárcel, estas prisiones, estos tormentos
que yo instalo en la mitad de mis poemas.

Perdonadme hermanos estos recuentos.
Sucede que desde entonces, yo soy
memoria.

El árbol

Resulta que el hombre
más alegre del mundo,
es un hombre verde.

Es un árbol primaveral
con tendencia solar
y de veranos.

A veces le vi dorado
y otoñal, pero jamás triste
pues no tiene vocación
de inviernos.

Bajo su generosa copa
y cerca de sus pródigas

Forgive me

Forgive me for these sorrows that I retell
and repeat.

Forgive me for these funeral processions,
this confinement, these prisons, these torments
that I place in the midst of my poems.

Forgive me, my brothers, for this retelling.
It happens that, since then, I am but
memory.

A tree

It turns out that the most joyful
man in the world
is a man who is coloured green.

Like a tree sprouting in Spring
with a penchant for the sun
and for summertime.

I would sometimes see him in a golden light
and looking autumnal, but never sad
for he does not feel a commitment
towards winter.

Under his generous crown
and close to his bountiful

manos extendidas,
La gente se agrupa para
gozar del amor que se
derrama.
Por eso para mí también,
fue imposible no amarle.

Preguntas

Quién soy yo, además de esta pseudosombra
que balbucea en otras lenguas,
además de esta figura mal parada que oscila
en el espacio y se tambalea?

Quién soy yo, ahora que poco a poco
la memoria me desdice y me cortan los caminos
todas las fronteras de la tierra?

Quién soy yo, además de un cierto indeciso
candidato a ministro de la muerte,
a contadora de tumbas que no estén en
ningún cementerio?

protracted hands,
people gather to
rejoice in that overflowing love.
That is why it was also impossible for me
not to love him.

Questions

Aside from this deceptive shadow
that babbles in other languages,
aside from this dented contour that, staggering, wavers
in space, who am I?

Who am I, now that my memory gradually
disproves me, and the boundaries on this earth
curtail the routes I take?

Aside from a wavering candidate
to the post of minister of death, or to the post
of bookkeeper of tombs not to be found in any
graveyard, who am I?

Cierto temor

Hay cierto temor en el ojo
de las cosas,
un temblor en sus voces de madera,
impenetrables sólo se acercan a sí mismas,
y permanecen estables,
pero riéndose.
¡Así de malas pueden ser las cosas!
¡Ojo!

El último árbol

Con rigurosa exactitud
voy respondiendo a las pocas
cartas que aún me llegan.

Con rigurosa exactitud
considero los temas,
Los diálogos que podrían
haber sido si en lugar
de cartas pudiéramos
haber hablado.

Con rigurosa exactitud
me extiendo por ellos,
y voy diciéndome lo
que nadie nunca oirá.

A kind of fear

There is a kind of fear in the eye
of things,
a shudder in their wooden voices,
impenetrable as they are, getting closer only to themselves,
whilst remaining stable,
and yet they laugh.
Yes, things can be this bad!
 Stay alert!

The last tree

With punctilious precision,
I will reply to the few letters I
still get in the post.

With punctilious precision,
I reflect on the various subjects that could have been discussed
and on the exchanges
that could have taken place,
had we spoken to each other
instead of writing letters.

With punctilious precision,
I expand on those dialogues, saying to myself
all those things that no one
will ever hear me say.

Con rigurosa exactitud van
así naciendo nuevos diálogos,
nuevos temas, ramas mayores
de comunicación que no será.
Y así de pronto crece,
está entero ante mí,
el implacable árbol
de la soledad.

With punctilious precision,
new dialogues are thus born,
fresh subjects, greater branches of
communication that will never come to be.
And abruptly it develops, wholly emerging in front of me,
the implacable, relentless tree
of solitude.

EDUARDO EMBRY
(Chile)

Eduardo Embry was born in Valparaíso, Chile, in 1938. In 1969 he published the poetry collection *Poeta en Valparaíso*, shortlisted for the Concurso Internacional de Casa de las Américas. After the 1973 *coup d'état*, he was a political prisoner aboard the ship Lebu.

Upon his release, he received an invitation from the University of Glasgow, and in 1974 he left for the UK, where he taught in Scotland, Southampton and Bournemouth. He later travelled to Venezuela, residing in the city of Cumaná, in Sucre State, where he conducted specialist research for the Deanship of Universidad de Oriente; he was also the coordinator for cultural events at the Ateneo in Cumaná.

When he returned to the UK, he resumed his teaching career, being the recipient of several awards. In 2011, he was awarded the prize given by Círculo de Críticos de Arte de Valparaíso. He has produced a vast body of work comprising twenty-five books.

Eduardo Embry nació en 1938 en Valparaíso, Chile. En 1969 se publicó una selección de sus poemas bajo el título Poeta en Valparaíso, *finalista en el Concurso Internacional de Casa de las Américas. Tras el Golpe de Estado de 1973, fue prisionero político en el buque Lebu.*

Liberado, recibe una invitación de la Universidad de Glasgow y en 1974 parte a Inglaterra, donde ejerció la docencia en Escocia, Southampton y Bournemouth. Más adelante viajó a Venezuela, instalándose en la ciudad de Cumaná, en el Estado Sucre, donde realizó trabajos especiales para el Decanato de la Universidad de Oriente; y fue coordinador de actividades culturales del Ateneo de Cumaná.

De regreso en Reino Unido, retomó su carrera docente recibiendo varias distinciones, y en 2011, recibió el Premio otorgado por el Círculo de Críticos de Arte de Valparaíso.

Su vasta obra comprende hasta la actualidad más de 25 libros.

Noticias de última hora

A punto estaba de cerrar las conexiones,
de poner en forma segura el corazón en reposo,
una de las 25 letras del teclado
viene corriendo, a gritos pide que no cierre,
que no,

me trae las últimas noticias de la tarde,
los nevados de la Antártica
se convierten en harina pan;
la Ronkita, persona amorosa de mis versos,
me dice, nadie consume pescado,
se teme a la marea roja;

una mujer recibe una paliza,
con violencia le arrancan los ojos;
aunque no estamos viviendo los tiempos de Odiseo,
por una sola mujer golpeada
yo me iría a la guerra;

mi corazón, por ahora, no reposa.

De los hechos ridículos

Lo que excita en nosotros la risa
es ver algo feo,
o lo bruscamente deforme;
pero, desde algún tiempo
a esta parte, me río

Last minute news

And as I was about to shut down all connections,
and safely place the heart at rest,
one of the 25 letters on the keyboard
rushes towards me and yells, begging me not to do it,
please don't

it brings me the latest news from that afternoon,
the snows in Antarctica
are turning into bread flour;
Ronkita, that loving person in my poems,
tells me that no one eats fish anymore,
people are afraid of the red tide;

a woman is battered,
her eyes are violently gouged out;
we are not living in the days of Odysseus
but then for a single battered woman
I would set off to war;

no, for now my heart cannot rest.

About ridiculous facts

What arouses laughter in us
is seeing something ugly
or that which is bluntly misshapen;
but for some time now, I laugh

ante la belleza
de las cosas sencillamente perfectas,
me río
hasta de las gotas de agua
que se deslizan sobre
el vidrio de la ventana,
con mayor razón,
me río de los árboles
pegados a la tierra
¿qué habrán hecho de malo estos bribones
que dios los dejó ahí quietecitos?,
cuando nos marchamos
a la playa, apenas se mueven
para decirnos con sus ramas "adiós, adiós,
que les vaya bien",
nosotros, para ganar tiempo,
para poner las sillas patas arriba,
pasamos veloces
dejando atrás la casa,
los pollitos, la ropa tendida,
el puente y los árboles;
la perfección del sol que gira,
así como lo pintan los niños,
alegre mamarracho amarillo ardiendo,
ojos, nariz y boca grande,
nos hace reír a carcajadas.

at the beauty of things that are
simply perfect,
I even laugh at the drops of water
gliding on the windowpane,
and justifiably I laugh at the
trees stuck to the ground,
what have these rascals done wrong, for God
to leave them there as still as can be?
when we leave to go to the beach, they faintly move
their branches to say to us: "Bye-bye, enjoy yourselves!"
and to save time
placing the chairs upside down, we walk by quickly
leaving behind our house,
the tiny chicks, the laundry
hanging from the clothes-line,
the bridge and the trees;
the rotating sun is nothing but perfection, just as a child
would draw it: a happy yellow
scorching jerk that has eyes
and a nose and a large mouth,
it makes us burst out laughing.

Antes de que [tú] encendieras la TV

Estoy pensando - en la peligrosa etapa crítica que está viviendo Europa - los escritos de Malaparte relacionados con la crisis que provocó la Primera Guerra Mundial y su continuación en la Segunda, con tantos signos de crueldad y miseria que se están extendiendo por el mundo - leyendo, digo, a ese "raro" escritor italiano, republicano, fascista, seguidor de Musolini y de Hitler, que terminara convertido al comunismo pekinista - conocedor de aquel mundo - parece haber advertido "cuidado" británicos, hay que reforzar la idea comunitaria - que es la única forma de parar gobiernos autoritarios que han centrado su actuación en el odio al extranjero, en la guerra y en el saqueo de los caudales nacionales. En esto estaba pensando antes de que el noticiario de la TV comenzara a transmitir una versión distinta
de lo que había pasado en la guerra.

Versos de entretención en el encierro

Nadie pregunta quién eres
de dónde vienes, para dónde vas,
las orejas se ponen alertas,
abren los ojos, porque la gente aprende
o de lo que oye o de lo que enseñan los golpes,

por eso es que las orejas se ponen rojas,
los ojos se cierran y las manos,
que son históricamente las partes
del cuerpo humano que mejor construyen,
con mayor eficiencia que las orejas,
la boca y los dientes,

Before you switched on the TV

And so I am reflecting – on the dangerous and critical stage that Europe is going through – on the writings of Malaparte regarding the crisis that triggered the First World War and which continued during the Second World War, with so many signs of cruelty and misery spreading all over the world – and as I was saying, when reading that the texts of that "rare" Italian writer, a republican, a fascist, a follower of Mussolini and Hitler, who ended up converting to Beijing communism – an expert on the subject of that particular world – he seems to have warned the British people that the idea of community must be reinforced – it is the only way to stop authoritarian governments who have focused their efforts on hatred towards foreigners, on war and on the looting of national wealth. Yes, I was reflecting about all those things before the newsreel began to broadcast a different version of what had happened in the war.

Entertaining verses during lockdown

Nobody asks you who you are
where you are from, where you are going,
your ears are on alert
and your eyes are well open, and this is because you learn
either from what you hear or from what you are taught by the blows
you have received

that is why ears turn red,
eyes shut and hands –historically
the parts of the human body that are best
built– so much more efficient than ears,
mouth and teeth,

pero nunca mejor que los ojos
de una muchacha que se enamora a primera vista,
es por aquellas dos luminarias
del proverbio que dice del bienaventurado
que donde pone el ojo
pone amor a todas las cosas que toca:

con la boca y la lengua
se sensibilizan las flores,
se agudiza la piel de los animales;

con los dientes se muerden las uvas,
con la pulpa crujiente de la sandía,
se embetuna la cara y el cabello;

no así los peces, ni los perros, ni los gatos,
tampoco los inteligentes delfines;
con hilo y aguja se repara o altera la ropa,
se crean nuevas prendas de vestir;
vamos a ver si puedo explicarlo todo
con una sola palabra, como una sola ciruela
sin olvidar el dolor ni la sangre,
se fabrican máquinas de coser
se hacen almohadas, y de un
solo ribete bien pronunciado,
viva la nueva constitución!
se hace volar los árboles,
los pájaros que saben cuándo
es lunes o cuándo es domingo,
van pegados a sus ramas.

but never truer than the eyes of
a young woman who falls in love at first sight,
such are the two beacons of the proverb stating
that blessed are those who, whatever they set their eyes on,
offer love to whatever they touch:

with mouths and tongues
flowers are aroused,
animal hide is heightened;
teeth bite grapes,
and with the crisp flesh of watermelons
face and hair end up tarred;

this is not the case with fish, dogs, or cats,
nor with clever dolphins;
clothes are mended or transformed with thread and needle,
and new garments are made;
let us see if I can explain it all
with a single word, as if it were a single plum,
without forgetting the pain and the bloodshed:
sewing machines are manufactured
and pillows are produced, and from a well-uttered
embellishment,
long live the new constitution!
Trees blowing up
yet birds fly close to their branches,
whether it is Monday or Sunday,
what do they know?

¿Sientes tú lo mismo que yo?

Mi cuerpo se extiende,
mi cuerpo se enrosca,
mi cuerpo se incendia,
mi cuerpo enroscado teme
se convierta en cenizas sobre tu cuerpo
mi cuerpo teme que sople el viento,
de mis cenizas, de tus cenizas
no quede nada.

¿Qué es la dialéctica?

De tanto oír esa palabra,
siguiendo el consejo de un sabio chino,
salí a la calle para hacer una encuesta
con una sola pregunta:
¿qué entiende usted por dialéctica?

algunos se encogían de hombros
para decir delicadamente, no lo sé
otros de modo directo como un puñetazo,
dijeron "¡ándate al diablo!";
pero la respuesta que más me satisfizo,
fue la que dio Penélope:
¿qué entiende usted por dialéctica?
"es una forma de pensar como un espiral
en que las palabras simples se alargan
y las más complicadas se vuelven
más tiernas que un gato."

Do you feel the same as I do?

My body spreads,
my body twirls,
my body catches fire,
my curled-up body is afraid
of becoming ashes over your body
my body dreads the wind blowing,
and from my ashes and your ashes
nothing will remain.

What is Dialectics?

Having heard that word ever so many times, I followed the advice
of a Chinese sage, and so I went out
into the streets to carry out a survey
that was to include but a single question:
What do you understand by the term Dialectics?

Several people shrugged their shoulders to convey,
oh ever so delicately, that they had no idea.
A few others answered with the directness
of a thump on my jaw: "Go to hell!"
But the reply that delighted me most was what
Penelope said when I asked her: What do you understand by the term
Dialectics, Penelope? And she replied:
"It's a mode of thinking, comparable to a spiral along which
plain words are lengthened, whilst the more complex words become
gentler than a cat."

DIEGO FLORES-JAIME
(México)

Diego Flores-Jaime was born en 1965, in Monterrey, Mexico. Since 1990, he is a Lecturer in Spanish Literature and Translation at *University College London*. He has published the poetry collection *Alud de la sal* (1998); *Between Two Worlds: Poetry & Translation*, a recording from the *British Library* (2009); and a second poetry collection *Adversarias* (2019). He is also a contributor to several media, such as the newspapers *El Norte*, *El Porvenir* and *La Jornada*. At present, he is working on a book about his travels through South East Asia.

Diego Flores-Jaime nació en 1965 en Monterrey, México. Trabaja como profesor de lengua española y traducción en University College London desde 1990.
Ha publicado Alud de la sal *(poesía) 1998;* Between Two Worlds: Poetry & Translation *(grabación de la British Library), 2009; Adversarias (poesía), 2019. Además de colaboraciones periodísticas en diversos medios tales como los periódicos* El Norte, El Porvenir *y* La Jornada. *Prepara un libro sobre viajes a través del sureste asiático.*

Esto de abrir y vuélvete no es el látigo
El chispazo de los días en que palidecer
Tiene otro sentido
(no la iluminación, el alumbramiento)
Hablo de algo que no alcanza a divisar el faro
Una presencia,
Una antorcha incendiando los puños
Un ladrillo y otro,
Qué poca luz
Para explicarlo todo

Esto de abrir es una ausencia
Vertida donde voy cercando al muro:
Siglo coronado de bujías
Una revelación darás a sombra

Vete de bruces, aprende el haz: sangra
Es centelleo lo que escurre
Hilos de luz que lamen la penumbra

Esto de abrir y dar vuelta a la noria
Inflama la mañana, llaga, cala
Los huesos y revienta las heridas

Olvidadizo el día que acontece
Gris, sin una trémula, pálida luz
En el umbral de la puerta sagrada
de una taberna tuve la virtud
de no olvidar mi fracaso
Bebí penosamente para alcanzar la lucidez
Equilibrando el camino que va
de la mesa a la letrina

This business of opening and turning around is not a whip
The spark of days in which going pale
has another meaning
(neither illumination nor giving birth)
I am talking about something that cannot quite make out the lighthouse
A presence,
A flare igniting your fists
A brick and another brick,
There's not enough light
to explain it all

This business of opening is an absence
Spilt along where I am surrounding that partition:
A century crowned with sparks
A reveal in the shade, thou shalt give

Fall flat on your face, grasp the beam: it bleeds
What drains glimmers
Threads of light licking the twilight

This business of opening and going around the waterwheel
The morning ignites, a sore, it soaks
to the bone and makes wounds burst

So forgetful is the day born grey
without a tremulous, pale light

On the threshold of the sacred door
of a tavern I had the advantage of not
forgetting my failures
I drank gallingly to attain clarity
Balancing the path that leads from the table

a medio andar
entre este vaso y el otro
lejos del llanto y de la risa
Todavía sobrio, desolado en el centro
de la isla de la soberbia
tuve la vergüenza de escribir unos versos
Alejado ya de toda virtud
me vi salir
casi feliz de conservar la sed

¿Qué se hace con la mujer
de bella cabeza, en el centro
del jardín, sentada y lejos
de la rosa que a fuerza
de ser se vuelve pétalo?
Huyó el instante, la visión
lastimándote los ojos. Llega
la noche colgada de la trenza
de las niñas, hartas ya de crecer
en el inicio de la hora de la siesta
¿Qué se hace con la luz
si no se tiene un desván
un ático vacío, triste
ya sin polvo?

to the latrine
half-walking
between this glass and that one
away from weeping and laughing
Still sober, but desolate in the middle
of an island of conceit
I had the nerve to write a few verses
devoid of all virtue
I saw myself leave
almost happy to be hanging on to my thirst

What to do with a woman
who boasts a beautiful head, in the middle
of the garden, sitting down and away
from a rose that by just being itself
turns into a petal?
Immediately fleeing, that vision
hurts your eyes. Night enters
dangling from the tresses of girls, tired as they are
of growing up
now that the afternoon nap has just begun.

What to do with the light
if you lack a space under eaves, an
empty and sad-looking attic now that it
has been dusted?

Preguntar es inútil ejercicio,
la luz se ha vuelto amarga
y la mujer: ¿Quién sabe?

El escribiente es el desamor
Amamos de la escritura su virtud
Nada nos contiene ni nos habita
Volcado el desamor sobre el cajón del vacío
Un hueco sordo
Oscuro que no acallará la noche
El desamor del escribiente
Estas líneas perplejas tras el beso
Obsceno el hacedor, el escribiente obsceno
Se tira al rio de la escritura
Para romperse la cara
Añicos que ningún oleaje dispersa
Escritura que se describe
Y al dibujarse se desnuda
El amor es el desamor
Es la piel del suicida vuelta del revés
Vuelta de nuevo
Y que no es lo mismo
Se desdibuja el desamor
En las mismas aguas donde fue creado
El escribiente es el desamor
Y la pluma al vuelo

Asking questions is a useless exercise,
the light has become bitter,
and the woman, who knows?

Disaffection is a scribe
From the act of writing we love its virtue
Nothing contains us or lives within us
Disaffection dumped into the drawer of emptiness
A dull gap
So dark that it will not silence the night
The disaffection of the scribe
Such perplexing lines after a kiss
Obscene is the maker, and obscene is the scribe
Throwing himself into the river of writing
to bust his face
Such are the shards that no surf can disperse
Writing describing itself,
Displaying its nudity as it is drawn.
Love is disaffection
It is the skin of those who commit suicide
Turned the other way round
And round again
Which is not the same
Disaffection is blurred
within the exact waters where it was created
The scribe is disaffection
the writing pen in mid-air

Habrase visto la ventana
el parpadeo del tren
quebrando la esquina: ese furor
y más furor donde las piernas
y esa equis enorme que no sabe
Y si sabe, maldice!
al horizonte el saber
la pantallita de muchos
vómito que no me trago
reverencia inútil
efervescencia de la reflexión
No hablo de un pensar profundo
sino de la luz que cala
aqui
    allí
       entre nos
que decimos y callamos

Voy a tocar la puerta del deseoso
el humeante
que imaginé un barco calafateado
que no tocase tierra
Suspenso en el aire
hediondo de mar afuera

Todavía oigo caer el polvo
Sobre los brazos de las estatuas
Los pechos de la muchacha
La lluvia, la ebriedad de los amigos

Aún veo los ojos de los árboles
Despeñándose en la acera

Hark at the window
the blinking of a train
turning the corner: that rage
and further rage of legs
and a gigantic X that does not know
And if it does know, it curses!
knowledge there in the horizon
the little screen of so many
I will not swallow that vomit
a hopeless curtsey
the effervescence of a reflection
I am not talking about profound thoughts
but about the light that suffuses
here
    there
       between us
both saying things and remaining silent

I will knock on the door of the wistful
of the smouldering
I imagined a caulked ship
that never reached land
Suspended in the air
foul-smelling at sea
I can still hear the dust falling
on the arms of statues
The girl's breasts
The rain, my intoxicated friends

I can still see the eyes of trees
falling headlong on the pavement
The wind pulling them down the street

El viento jalándolos calle abajo
El llanto, las hojas de Madre
Sin tinta ni pañuelos

Todavía las escobas, la escalinata urgida
El corredor, pasos en el desván
Me guiñan, entre el rumor: todavía

Es el polvo que entre mirar
Y escucha busca la salida

Incluso aún es todavía, oigo
Que dicen junto al afán del trapo

Concibo a mis hijas

Concibo a mis hijas
como a esas adversarias
que no cejan
pertinaces
como a esos días
implacables
de invierno

Así las concibo
como quien dice alborada
y no hay café con leche

Como quien espera

Weeping, Mother's pages
with neither ink nor handkerchiefs

The brooms are still there, the goaded staircase
The corridor, the steps leading to the loft
they wink, amid rumours: still now

The dust that, between watching and
listening, is looking for the exit

As of yet
it is still now, and I can hear
what they say
alongside the eagerness for rags

I think of my daughters

I think of my daughters
as adversaries
who do not let up
unrelenting
just like those
merciless
winter days

That is how I think of them
as someone announcing dawn
but then there is no white coffee

As someone waiting for the

al cartero
y no asoma el ratón
el inquilino

Concibo a mis hijas
como a una sinfonía
de cucharas

Como un estruendo
Como un susurro
las concibo

Imperturbable

E1 otoño seguía pudriéndonos
amoroso en la hurnedad
profunda
como cuando abrazamos
y el abrazo es vacío
es lengua inexistente
imposible de traducir

El otoño no es otra cosa
sino hojas
hijas ruidosas
bajo nuestros pies
adversarias
que coronará el invierno

Música viva

postman
and yet the tenant
shows not even a mouse

I think of my daughters
as a symphony
of spoons

Like a roar
Like a whisper
that is how I think of them

Composed

Autumn went on making us rot
though it was loving in that deep
dampness
as when we embrace
and the clinch is hollow
like an inexistent language
that would be impossible to translate

Autumn is nothing
but leaves
loud daughters
under our feet
adversaries
that will crown Winter

Live music

en las azoteas
donde el musgo
es amarilla alfombra

Ya no son hojas
Lo que engaña a los ojos

Imperturbable otoño
púdrete en la felicidad
del invierno

Desamparo

hermoso invierno
por la mañana
trajo la nieve
y el desamparo

del árbol pende
la cuerda
el cuello
mi cuello en soga
es esa cuerda que me recuerda
dolor de garganta
y sin tequila

el desamparo
gallo perdido
desafinado
nunca es temprano

on rooftops
where moss
is a yellow carpet

Those things deceiving our eyes
are no longer leaves

Composed autumn,
decay away in winter's
happiness

Helplessness

during the morning
that beautiful winter
brought with it both snow
and helplessness

from the tree hangs
the rope
the neck
my neck in a noose
that is the rope reminding me
of a sore throat
without a drop of tequila

helplessness
like a lost rooster
out of tune
it is never too early

para el canto del gallo mudo

la cama suave
se queda sola
sin nuestros cuerpos

y el desamparo
y el desamparo
sigue desnudo
sigue temblando
sabe del sol
lo echa de menos
es extrañeza
no desamparo
el desamparo

for the crowing of a muted rooster

the softest bed
remains on its own
deprived of our bodies

and helplessness
and helplessness
is still bare
is still trembling
it knows about the sun
missing it
it is then longing
not helpless
helpless

LESTER GÓMEZ MEDINA
(Nicaragua-Costa Rica)

Lester Gómez Medina was born in Nicaragua, and he is a Costa Rican national. He has a degree in Spanish Philology from the University of Costa Rica. In 2014 he came to the United Kingdom and developed a keen interest in short story writing and poetry. He currently lives in the UK. In 2018, he completed an MA in Audiovisual Translation at the University of Roehampton. In 2018, he took part in Invisible Presence, a project to nurture and develop writers of Latin American background. In 2021, he was selected to work with poet Jane Duran, which resulted in his first poetry collection *The Riddle Of The Cashew*, which was published by Exiled Writers Ink (EWI).

Lester Gómez Medina es de nacionalidad costarricense, y origen nicaragüense. Estudió Filología Española en la Universidad de Costa Rica. Se interesó seriamente por la escritura de relatos y poesía después de llegar a Inglaterra en 2014, donde vive actualmente. En 2018, completó una maestría en Traducción Audiovisual en la Universidad de Roehampton (Inglaterra).
En 2018, participó como miembro del programa de desarrollo de escritores Invisible Presence. En 2021, fue seleccionado para trabajar con la poeta Jane Duran, fruto de esto fue su primera colección de poemas, The Riddle Of The Cashew, *publicado por la organización Exiled Writers Ink, de la cual actualmente es miembro de la junta directiva.*

El polvo de mi casa

Mi padre nació muerto.
Vi a mi hermana mayor frotarse los ojos,
'Tengo polvo', decía.

¿A quién se parecía? pregunté.
'No importa.' Respondió mi otra hermana.
El polvo flotaba en el aire.

La una a la otra se decía, 'Sopla en mi ojo.'
Yo quise ayudarlas,
pero siempre me dijeron 'No importa'.

A veces visito a mis hermanas,
cuando la mayor me ve llegar
comienza a frotarse los ojos.

El hijo pródigo

Cuando dejó la ciudad
        no tuvo miedo de convertirse en sal,
mirar atrás ni siquiera fue una opción,
        desde la ventanilla del avión vio las luces,
unas amarillentas otras más claras
        dibujando el relieve del valle, las montañas,
luces como manos diminutas agitándose.

Las alas del avión le hicieron pensar en ángeles
        los que nunca vio, pero supo que vuelan,

The dust at home

My father was born dead.
I saw my older sister rubbing her eyes,
'It's dust', she would say.

Who did it look like? I asked.
'It doesn't matter,' my other sister said.
The dust floated in the air.

One sister would say to the other: 'Blow into my eye.'
I wanted to help them
but they always replied: 'It doesn't matter.'

I sometimes visit my sisters,
when the older one sees me arriving
she starts to rub her eyes.

The prodigal son

When he left the city
          he was not afraid of becoming a statue of salt,
looking back was not even an option,
          from the plane's porthole he saw the lights,
some yellow and others of a lighter colour
          tracing the silhouette of the valley and mountains,
lights as tiny hands waving.

The wings of the plane reminded him of angels,
          those he never saw but knew they could take flight,

los que nunca oyó, pero supo que cantan,
          como los querubines, que siempre cantan
y sintió pena por ellos, pues no logró entender
          para qué cantar y cantar cuando hay en la vida,
finita o eterna, tanto qué vivir y andar.

Piso de tierra

Escuché
que la vieja casa de ladrillos rojos donde nací
                    finalmente cedió.
                    El techo,
exhausto ya de las tejas, se vino abajo.
                    Pobre,
                    tanto sol y tanta lluvia,
tanto sostener la ilusión de que uno volviera.

Escuché
que fue de noche, que tronaron las alfarjías,
                    de golpe
                    cayeron las tejas.
Cuanto aguante, cuanta vida,
                    tanto esperar
                    a que uno otra vez la viera.
Lástima, pues lo usual es que uno atienda

                    a ver los restos,
                    a cerrar ese capítulo.
Escuché

those he never heard, but knew they would chant
      like cherubs, who are always chanting
and he felt sorry for them, for he never managed to understand
     why so much chanting and chanting when in life,
whether finite or eternal, there are so many things to live for
    so many paths to tread.

Dirt floor

I heard
that the old red-brick house where I was born
         finally gave way.
         The roof toppled,
tired as it was of the rooftiles.
         Poor old thing,
         so much sun and so much rain,
for so long dreaming that I would return.

I heard
that it happened at night, the battens thundered,
         and abruptly
         the rooftiles toppled.
So much endurance, so much life,
         waiting for so long
         for me to see it once again.
A shame really, because the usual thing is for people to go and see
         what remains
         and close that chapter.

I heard

que no se encontró a nadie
             bajo los escombros.
El estruendo sacudió al barrio,
             luego todo quedó en silencio.

El día de la iguana

Tuve que rehacer mi relación con mi madre
             tantas veces que llegué a pensar
              no íbamos a lograr mucho después de todo.

Si ella pensaba que yo le había desobedecido,
             El castigo venía sobre mí, una y otra vez.
                     Nunca decía lo siento.

         Llegué a creer
                 que seguía molesta
                     con mi padre.

Una mañana ella salió de casa,
         a vender productos porcinos.
                 Yo estaba en el patio

apaleando a una iguana,
         'Dejá de lastimar al pobre animal,'
                 gritó tío Juan.

that no one was found
           under the rubble.
The roar shook the neighbourhood,
           and then all was silent.

The day of the iguana

I had to rebuild the relationship with my mother so many times
      that I decided that
      we would not achieve much in the end.

If she thought I had disobeyed her,
      The punishment came upon me over and over again.
          I would never say I was sorry.

      I came to believe
          that she was still upset
             with my father.

One morning she left home,
      to sell pork products.
          I was in the yard

beating up an iguana,
      'Stop hurting the poor animal,'
          uncle Juan shouted.

Yo tenía unos ocho o nueve años,
      confundido, tratando de entender por qué
          Juan me había regañado,

yo lo había visto destazar un cerdo
      cada fin de semana. Yo reproché,
          'De cualquier manera, mamá la va a matar.'

Juan guardó silencio y me miró.
      Con voz calma dijo, 'Esa no es la manera.'
          Años más tarde, por primera vez,

mi madre me pidió que la escuchara.
      Guardé silencio, y la miré,
Ella dijo, 'Perdoname.'

Mercedita bajo la lluvia de 1979

En memoria

La menor de mis tías
iba a cumplir quince.
Pidió un vestido y zapatos rosados.
Quería un día sin lluvia
para su fiesta de cumpleaños.

Si Sandino lo hubiera sabido
por ella habría cesado la lluvia,
aunque solo ese día,
como regalo a Mercedita;
pero al general ya lo habían destituido.

I was about eight or nine,
        feeling confused and trying to understand why
                Juan had scolded me,
I would see him butchering a pig
        every weekend. And I reproached him
            'Whatever you say, mum's going to kill it.'

Juan was silent and looked at me.
        He then said in a calm voice: 'That's not the way to do it.'
                Years later, for the first time,

my mother asked me to listen to her.
        I was silent and looked at her,
she finally said it: 'Forgive me.'

Mercedita under the rain of 1979

In memoriam

The youngest of my aunts
was about to be fifteen.
She asked for a dress and shoes in pink.
For her birthday party
she wanted a day without rain

If Sandino had known,
he would have stopped the rain for her,
even if only for a day,
as a present to Mercedita;
but the general had already been ousted.

Una noche a Mercedita le dio frío,
le llegó primero a las piernas,
dijo que no las sentía.
La lluvia le nubló la vista.
Mercedita oyó el cielo tronar,

escuchó un avión que pasaba,
la lluvia retumbó sobre las casas
como bombas de aviones, como rifles,
balas rebotando contra el techo
como agua escurriéndose en las casas

y la gente se mojaba,
se mojaba, Mercedita, como vos.

Quiero pedirles un favor

Ya no oren a Dios por mí, mi alma está perdida,
        se los pido yo, no el diablo poseyéndome
ni mi cultura ni ningún demonio,
        se los pide mi voz.

Los demonios nunca quisieron nada conmigo
        ellos saben que ya no doy tregua ni diezmo,
que llevo mis pecados y mis reproches
        en un saco para guardar mazorcas.

A Dios le avergüenza mi saco
        no se alude responsable
de que mis rodillas conocieran los granos de maíz

One night Mercedita felt a chill,
first along her legs,
she said she could not feel them.
The rain clouded her eyesight.
Mercedita heard thunder in the sky

a plane flying overhead,
the rain rumbled over the houses
like bombs from planes, or rifles,
bullets bouncing against the roof
water seeping inside the houses

and people got soaked,
they got soaked, Mercedita, just like you did.

I would like to ask you for a favour

Do not pray to God for me, my soul is lost,
      I beg you, it is not the devil possessing me
nor my culture nor any demons,
      it is my voice beseeching you.

Demons never wanted anything to do with me
      they know I give no truce nor tithe,
that I carry my sins and my rebukes
      in a sack where corncobs are kept.

God is ashamed of my sack
      yet claims no responsibility
about my knees becoming acquainted with grains of corn

contra el suelo en la esquina de un cuarto

con las manos colocadas para orarle a él
        para que alejara de mí la rebeldía
y los fantasmas que rodeaban mi casa,
        incluido mi padre.

Yo debía orar para ser purgado de la idea
        que la gente tiende a ser miserable
por imagen y semejanza de Dios.
        Pero qué le voy a hacer, no fui librado

y qué más da ser juzgado, al fin y al cabo, hay paz en entender
        por qué la sal arde en las heridas, como arde en el alma
la poesía, qué más da, haber sido un terco convencido
    que los cisnes son hermosos más por su bravura

que por su apariencia, qué más da ser
        creyente de que no hay zenzontle nicaragüense
ni yigüirro *costarricense ni* blackbird *británico*
        pues estas aves migran.

Ya no oren a Dios por mí, no digan que él me bendiga
        pues no hay remedio para mi alma perdida,
ni hay demonios, diablo, ni dios que entienda
a mi alma descarriada de poesía.

lying on the floor in the corner of a room

with hands ready to pray to him
        and ask him to drive my rebelliousness away from me
as well as the ghosts surrounding my house,
        even my father's shadow.

I was supposed to pray to flush out my belief
        that people tend to be miserable
in the image and likeness of God.
        But what can I do, I was not spared

and what difference does it make to be judged after all, there is peace in understanding
        why salt makes wounds burn, how poetry burns
inside your soul, and what does it matter if I was obstinate, convinced
    that if swans are beautiful, it is more for their bravery

than for their appearance, what difference does it make
        to believe that there is no such thing as a Nicaraguan *zenzontle*
or a Costa Rican *yigüirro* or a British *blackbird*,
        for these are all migrating birds.

Do not pray to God for me, do not ask him to bless me
        since there is no cure for my lost soul,
there are no demons, devils or gods who can understand
my soul, my errant soul for the sake of poetry.

La forma humana

La verdad
todavía es así,
como en aquel tiempo.
Se afana en tenernos con hambre,
adora sentirse escasa en la mesa.
Le llamamos
y no atiende,
le rogamos,
y es esquiva.

La mentira
en cambio, es más cumplida,
telaraña en los rincones de casa,
intrincada hija del arte.
Y nosotros,
cada quien en su teléfono.
Más que verdad, más que mentira,
somos
huesos disfrazados de carne
y ojos que dan lástima,
los
vuelve locos   la apariencia
no
lo que arde   en el alma.

The human form

The truth
is still like this,
as it was then.
It strives to keep us hungry,
it loves to make itself scarce when we are sitting at the table.
We call out to it
yet it does not arrive,
we implore it,
and it eludes us.

Lies, by contrast,
are so much more considerate,
a spiderweb in every corner of the house,
an intricate daughter of Art.
In the meantime, here we are,
each one of us on their phone.
More than the truth, more than lies,
we are
bones disguised as flesh
our eyes so pitiful,
appearances
makes them   go crazy
not
what burns   inside our soul.

ÓSCAR GUARDIOLA-RIVERA

(Colombia)

Óscar Guardiola-Rivera is a renowned author, political essayist and Professor of Philosophy. He lives in London. His recent works include the poetic novel *Night of the World*, the first part of a trilogy, published in 2020 by The87 Press, and *Kingdom Risen, Kingdom Fallen*, commissioned for the Royal Literary Fund and published in 2021 for WritersMosaic – the text is available here: *https://writersmosaic.org.uk/people/oscar-guardiola-rivera/*

Óscar Guardiola-Rivera es un destacado escritor, ensayista político y profesor de filosofía residente en Londres. Su obra reciente incluye la novela poética Night of the World, primera parte de una trilogía publicada en 2020 por The87 Press, y Kingdom Risen, Kingdom Fallen, parte de una comisión para el Royal Literary Fund publicado en 2021 por WritersMosaic y disponible en https://writersmosaic.org.uk/people/oscar-guardiola-rivera/

Variaciones sobre la línea cromática

Primer Tono

Un hombre cae desde la azotea
hasta el piso,
déjalo cayendo

Las sombras salen dejando tras de sí
la luz que les sirve de apoyo,
van desapareciendo

Queda la oscuridad del cuarto
y no puedes ver el volumen,
las aristas, los cristales,
el maderamen
los cobres

Un ligero resplandor anuncia una ventana
tras el cortinaje del lado derecho

Pero quedan los sonidos
ahí están los sonidos

Tienes que imaginar detrás de ellos

Debajo de ellos

Tienes que imaginar a Robert Fripp,
Phil Manzanera y Brian Eno

Variations on the chromatic line

First Tone

A man falls from the rooftop
to the ground,
let him fall

Shadows leave behind
the light providing backup,
and begin to disappear

What remains in the room is darkness
and you cannot distinguish the volume,
the edges, the glass,
the woodwork
the fragments of copper

A light glow proclaims a window
there, behind the curtains on the right side

But the sounds remain,
the sounds are there

You need to imagine what is behind them

Or under them

You need to imagine Robert Fripp,
Phil Manzanera and Brian Eno

Ellos no están ahí
Tienes que imaginarlos,
debajo de los sonidos.

Segundo Tono

La lámpara nos niega su escasa luz
el ojo se desplaza sobre el vértice
del piso hasta la puerta

sin detenerse

aprisa sobre el maderamen del techo
el cristal roto de las paredes
cosidas de nuevo en el espanto
de la serpiente enrollándose
alrededor del clavel azul

Déjala enrollándose

La hilera de libros cae sobre su cabeza
removiendo espéculos de polvo
visibles tan solo por el haz de luz que se cuela
por la hendidura del cortinaje,
se levantan y jamás van a caer

Déjalas levantándose

El ojo atraviesa los cristales
Y ve a lo lejos una ventana encendida
El incendio se levanta hasta el cielo

No, they are not there
You need to imagine them
under the sounds.

Second Tone

The lamp denies us its limited light
the eye travels over the apex
of the floor and all the way to the door

without once stopping

all along the woodwork on the ceiling it captures
the broken glass on the walls
sewn together again in the horror
of a snake coiling
around the blue carnation

Let it coil

The row of books tumbles on its head
stirring specula of dust, they are
visible only because of the beams of light slipping through
a slit in the curtains,
getting up and never falling

Let them get up

The eye runs through the glass
And sees a lit window in the distance
The blaze rises up to the sky

Flamas verdes contra el oscuro cielo

Déjalo quemarse,
Su asiento es el único asiento
Entre todos los asientos
Que se hunde bajo la tierra

Cierra los ojos.

Tercer Tono

El ángel se levanta raudo sobre la espesura
verde la espesura
el calor ha caído sobre mí
el sol escapa a mi visión corrupta,
vertiginoso

El ángel va cayendo sobre la verde espesura.

Cuarto Tono

El oriental construyó un laberinto
consistente en una sola línea recta larga
larga, larga se pierde en el infinito
sin principio ni fin el laberinto
¿Cómo se puede entrar o salir de la línea recta larga?

Green flames against dark skies

Let it burn.
Its seat is the only seat
Among all seats
That sinks below ground

Close your eyes.

Third Tone

The angel swiftly gets up from all that is overgrown
green is the thicket
the heat plummets over me
the sun avoids my corrupt vision,
vertiginous as it is

An angel is falling onto the green thicket.

Fourth Tone

He, an oriental man, built a labyrinth
comprising a single long straight line
long, so long that it is lost in infinity
a labyrinth with no beginning and no end,
How can you enter or leave behind that long straight line?

Quinto Tono

Abu Said en las salinas de Aldabia
Abu Said salinase en las arenas
de Aldabia
salino said aldabó las arenas
minúsculas de Aldabia
Abu saludó al Minús de Aldabia
Enterrando su frente en las arenas
frente al entierro
hundió su daga
juró vengarse del Minús déspota
de Aldabia
en la arena su déspora frente
dejó caer gotas de brillo
y esperó sentado con la daga en su mano
en las minúsculas arenas de Aldabia

Abu Said en diáspora salinal
huyó de Aldabia
juró dar muerte al déspota caído
espetó a los ancianos su callada
frente
su gesto árido mirando al piso
pasó a brillo de su daga
las gargantas secas de los ancianos.

Sexto Tono

La silla enfrente de sí gira sobre sí
cada doce parpadeos.

Fifth Tone

Abu Said in the salt mines of Aldabia
Abu Said salt mines in the sands
of Aldabia
saline Said knocked on the minuscule
sands of Aldabia
Abu greeted the Minús of Aldabia
Burying his forehead in the sands
the forehead, the burial
he sank his dagger
and swore vengeance to the despot Minús
of Aldabia
in the sand his desporic forehead
dripped shining droplets
and he awaited, sitting down, with the dagger in his hand
in the minuscule sands of Aldabia

Abu Said in a saline diaspora
fled from Aldabia
and swore to slay the fallen despot,
and barked out to the elders, his silent
forehead
looking downwards
with a lifeless expression
whilst the shine of his dagger cut through
the dry throats of the elders.

Sixth Tone

The chair across him spins
every twelve blinks of an eye.

Séptimo Tono

Es eso lo que confunde al sujeto
la silla
enfrente de sí
gira sobre sí
cada doce parpadeos
al tredécimo ya se encuentra dormido
perdido sobre su silla
sobre sí
hundiéndose bajo tierra
mientras estallan los cristales
de la ventana
y el viento helado se cuela,

Ocupando los tercios de la habitación

Luce desolada
La serpiente y el clavel azul
sobre la repisa arriba de su cama
una sima profunda
háse tragado el piso y la tabla,

las sombras ya se retiran
los sonidos se han pervertido,

Mejor es que no abras los ojos.

Seventh Tone

That is what confuses the subject
the chair
across him
spins on itself
every twelve blinks of an eye
and on the thirteenth, he is already asleep
misplaced on his chair
upon himself
sinking under the ground
as the glass from the windows
shatters
and the freezing wind gatecrashes,

And occupying two thirds of the room

Looking desolate
the snake and the blue carnation
on the shelf above his bed
like a deep chasm
swallowing both the floor and the table,

shadows are now withdrawing
sounds have been perverted,

It is best not to open your eyes.

Octavo Tono

Un Oscuro Demonio Dióscuro
Tocó al vuelo su mano
El velo cayó de su rostro
Ensangrentado
Su vientre se hundió tras el vértigo del viento helado,

Nada detendrá la caída.

Noveno Tono

Giacomo Casanova cubierto
por el polvo de los años
sordo grita al mundo
la trasúltima de sus historias,

Seis mil veces disfrutó la misma mujer
en una noche
la misma noche
en que cayeron los astros.

Eighth Tone

A Dark Demon Godly-dark
Touched his hand on the fly
The veil fell from his countenance
His bleeding belly
sank after the vertigo brought about by the freezing wind,

Nothing will stop the fall.

Ninth Tone

Giacomo Casanova covered
by the dust of years
deafly shouts at the world
the very last of his stories,

He enjoyed the same woman six
thousand times
the same night
the stars fell from the sky.

Décimo Tono

El ángel cae sobre la verde espesura
al encierro
cuando todos despiertan
cesa el movimiento rápido del ojo
la esfera del mundo se detiene
la silla ya no gira
los cristales se recomponen
el polvo cae
el suicida grita
Abu Said deja caer la daga
Sobre las minúsculas arenas de Aldabia

La lámpara aún se halla encendida.

Tenth Tone

The angel falls on the green thicket
in the midst of confinement
and when they all wake up
the rapid movement of the eye stops
the sphere of the world comes to a halt
the chair can no longer spin
the pieces of glass reassemble
dust falls
those committing suicide shout out
Abu Said lets the dagger drop
On the minuscule sands of Aldabia

The lamp is still alight.

SEBASTIÁN MONTES
(Colombia)

Sebastián Montes was born in Armenia, Colombia. He is a poet, novelist and translator, and he has lived in London since 2011. He has a degree in Literary Studies from Pontificia Universidad Javeriana in Bogotá and an MRes in Art Theory and Philosophy from the University of the Arts in London. Since2017 he works as a translator for the International Psychoanalytical Association (IPA).

Sebastián Montes, nacido en Armenia, Colombia, es un poeta, novelista y traductor residente en Londres desde el 2011. Es Profesional en Estudios Literarios de la Pontificia Universidad Javeriana de Bogotá y cuenta con una maestría en Filosofía y Teoría del Arte de la University of Arts London. En la actualidad se desempeña como traductor de la Asociación Psicoanalítica Internacional, para la cual trabaja desde el año 2017.

Dictadura

Se precisan tres formas transparentes del amor
para inventar un grito en esta Chile diurna
paridora de poetas,
la elegía en flor de un hálito doméstico
o el silencio austero de los torturados.

Para aquellos que en las cosas simples ven a Dios
bastaba una mordaza en la memoria
para hablar del hambre,
un par de cantos de tribuna
para hacerle himnos al dolor;

por ello se negó la entrada a los reductos de la gloria
a los cultores de ese rictus en cadencia
que contiene la resignación,
se negó el exilio de la noche
y el arduo cirineo sedicioso
para lavar la dura cruz de su vergüenza.

Entonces se salvaron los poetas bien paridos
                                   [por la tierra,
los bardos de la gesta cotidiana
y el duro pan de cada día,
los rostros del clamor al filo de los versos,
los Rojas,
los Lihn,
los Parra,
los Neruda.

Dictatorship

You would require three see-through forms of love
to devise a scream in this luminous Chile,
the breeder of poets,
the flowering elegy delivered with homegrown exhalations
or the austere silence of those who were tortured.

As to those who see God in the simplest things,
it sufficed with gagging their memory
when they spoke about hunger,
engaging in a couple of chants from the stands
as hymns dedicated to grief;

thus, the entrance to the strongholds of glory was denied to
those who cast the throbbing grimace
that forbearance holds,
and the exile of the night was refused to them too,
as were any selfless allies –demanding yet defiant– to help wash away
the pitiless cross of their shame.

And so it was that poets worthy of being born from this land
                              [were spared:
the bards of everyday feats
and our harshest daily bread,
their countenance displaying the outcry
at the edge of every stanza,
the Rojas,
the Lihns,
the Parras,
the Nerudas.

Relato de un artista ciego

Desconoce el Dow Jones
y los subterfugios de la macroeconomía
la ambigua fluctuación de los mercados
el precio exorbitante de un amor romántico

abdicó al óxido airado de la superficie
y en lo estrecho de los túneles del metro
prefiere el tiempo oblicuo de los trenes
la manera de callar que tienen los viajantes
el hombre que se ríe noche y noche
de la crisis de la humanidad

Tranquilo
parado en su rincón ante el cartel de Gucci
que el mundo nunca ignora
tienta las entrañas del vacío con su bastón blanco
y silba melodías dulces
engalanado en su camino hacia la muerte

a quienes pagan con silencio lo delicado de su aire
voces puras hablan al oído del dolor humano
otros
arrojan metales devastados
a lo profundo de su oscuridad

es así como llegado el fin de cada acto
sus silbos apagados
se alejan como trenes
y nuevas formas se perciben
en una aritmética imperfecta

The Story of a Blind Artist

He is not aware of the Dow Jones
and the ploys of Macroeconomics
nor does he know about the ambiguous fluctuations of markets
or the exorbitant price of romantic love

he has relinquished aerated surfaces
and, along narrow subway tunnels,
he prefers the slanting time of trains and
the way travellers remain silent,
he, the man who laughs night in and night out
about the crisis experienced by humanity

Keeping calm,
standing in a corner, in front of a Gucci poster
that the world cannot ignore,
he senses the entrails of emptiness with his white cane
whilst whistling sweet melodies,
festooned as he is en route to his death

there are those who pay with silence for the frailness of his manner:
the purest voices speak into the ear of human suffering and
there are others
who throw distressed pieces of metal
into the depths of darkness

and this is how,
when reaching the end of each act,
his subdued whistling
recedes just like trains do
and takes on new shapes

es por ello que despertar al fondo de la noche
será materia siempre viva de su arte

Visiones del mendigo

Ando de pobre Cristo a tu recuerdo
clavado, reclavado...
Juan Gelman

Yo te vi pasar veloz
–color frutal de algún país lejano–
empujando las formas de la tarde
hacia la vera polvorienta del camino:
Era mi tránsito hacia el reino de los astros minerales.
Entonces quise urdir en aire
el hálito moral de tu respiración,
singlar un fuego etéreo
en horas de voracidad febril.

Pero habrían sido innumerables
los días con sus noches
errando en ese juego indócil
de espejos contrapuestos
–tentado a diluir aquel silencio lujurioso
que extendía sus raíces para sofocarme–.

¿Y qué habría sido entonces
buscar a aquel geómetra sutil,
el hombre que pudiera reinventar un hombre
y con él su corazón vibrátil?

into an imperfect arithmetic

and this is why
waking up in the depths of the night
will always be living raw material for his art

A beggar's visions

I am but the lowliest Christ beseeching your memory,
nailed to the cross, and nailed yet again...
Juan Gelman

I saw you passing by at speed
–the colour of fruit from some far away country–
thrusting the shapes that the afternoon takes
towards the dusty roadside:
It was my passage towards the kingdom of celestial, inanimate bodies.
And at that point I wished to weave in the air
the decorous panting of your breathing,
an unearthly fire sailing on a fixed course
at those moments of feverish voraciousness.

But days and their nights
would have been too many to count
when
wandering in that unruly game
of conflicting mirrors
–I was tempted to dilute the lustful silence that
spread its roots to stifle me.

And what then of looking
for that elusive surveyor,

Yo te vi pasar veloz
–hervor frugal de sangre indígena–
como atada a un ave fatigada,
traída por las avenidas.

Vida zen

Y si me fuera dado el don
escogería ser ciprés
y me mudaría al norte.
Moriría cien
o ciento cinco veces con el fin de cada año
para reinventarme con la primavera.
O me iría al sur
para ser yarumo en las montañas
y hacer así mi cuerpo
el hogar de un ruiseñor.
Sería savia de una ceiba
o piedra que atestigua desde el fondo
el curso milenario de su río.

No sabría entonces
qué es el Rivotril
ni el Diazepam
ignoraría los televisores
y las salas de espera
los domingos a la tarde
la mañana de los lunes
sí me fuera dado el don

the man who could reinvent another man
and alongside him his vibrating heart?

I saw you passing by at speed
–indigenous blood at boiling point, unadorned –
as if tied to the weariest fowl,
carried all along avenues.

Zen Life

And if I could make a wish
I would choose to be a Cypress Tree
and I would move North.
I would die a hundred times,
or even a hundred and five times when the year ended
so that I could recreate myself anew in Spring.
Or I would go South
and become a Trumpet Tree in the mountains
so that my body would be home to a nightingale.
I would be sap for a Kapok Tree, or a pebble
witnessing the river's age-old course
from the riverbed.

I would not know then
what Rivotril
or Diazepam were,
I would ignore TV sets
and waiting rooms
Sunday afternoons
Monday mornings
if I could make a wish

London Warning

Es la hora en que la reina toma el té
y hay un niño nepalí
que ve girar el mundo en una lavadora,
los blancos trenes del progreso humean en la lejanía
con sus vientres repletos de banqueros,
las botas de un soldado rubio
acarician dulcemente
las mejillas de una viuda afgana.

Es la hora en que la reina toma el té
y ríe el hombre ebrio de narcosis
que habla de amor a las vitrinas,
se extingue aquel caudal secreto
donde viejos pordioseros lavaron su tristeza
y ladra un perro enfermo
descifrando el acertijo de su rostro
para no beber el agua sucia de su espejo.

A la hora en que la reina toma el té,
como una mariposa indócil
que el silencio en pleno vuelo despedaza,
caen las formas minerales de la noche
para llenarse de artificio,
sangra un alguacil por boca y por espada
con su sonrisa laboral de los martes a la noche
en medio de un asalto carnicero.

Pero pasará la hora en que la reina toma el té
como pasan los aviones
y los cortejos funerarios

London Warning

It is tea-time for the Queen
and there is a Nepali child
who sees the world go round inside a washing-machine
white trains of progress emit smoke in the distance
with their bellies full of bankers,
the boots of a blond soldier
sweetly caress
the cheeks of an Afghani widow.

It is tea-time for the Queen
and the drunkard in a state of stupor
talks of love to shop-windows,
and the secret stream where old hobos
washed their sadness is now extinguished, and
a sick dog barks
decoding the conundrum in its muzzle
so as not to drink from the mirror of
those dirty waters

It is tea-time for the Queen,
and just like an unruly butterfly
silently ripped to pieces in mid-flight,
those mineral arrangements of the night plunge
as they engulf all with their ruse,
and in the midst of a bloodbath a policeman
can be seen bleeding from his mouth and
from his back, putting on the working smile
reserved solely for Tuesday nights.

But tea-time for the Queen will pass,

para que los ríos de la tarde desemboquen
y un rumor de tierra se perciba por las avenidas;
llegará la ira verdadera y el ensueño,
la vida estrepitosa de los niños multiformes
que ahogarán su sed con la miel de todo un Ganges.

like planes fly past
and like funeral processions drive by,
so that evening rivers will disgorge and tremors
will be felt all along avenues;
and thus, a veritable wrath will make way as well as reveries,
as will the rowdy life of children in their many forms
quenching their thirst with honey from a river as magnificent as the Ganges.

ALBERTO PAUCAR CÁCERES
(Perú)

Alberto Paucar Cáceres, *albertopaucarpoesia.com/* was born in Tarata, Tacna, Peru, in 1952. He has a degree in Industrial Engineering from Universidad Nacional de Ingeniería in Peru, as well as MAs from Mexico, Lancaster and Warwick universities, and a PhD from Manchester Metropolitan University, where he is currently a professor. He has lived in Manchester since 1987. His books include *Experto en Soledades* (1978); *A la caza del eterno ciervo* (1983); *Temporal de Ausencias* (1985); *Velero de humo abandona el reino* (1993); *Oficios de Trovador* (Peru, 2006); *Las flores de tu boca* (2009); *Cuaderno del Fauno* (2017); *Pícaro Monje, Mal de no verte* and *Poemas sobre el Atlántico* (e-books-2018); and *Obra Reunida* (UNJBG-2018). His latest book: *Del porfiado fauno y sus desamores en tiempos de pandemia* will be published in 2023.

Alberto Paucar Cáceres, *albertopaucarpoesia.com/ nació en Tarata, Tacna, Perú en 1952. Hizo estudios de ingeniería industrial en la Universidad Nacional de Ingeniería de Perú; Masters en México; Lancaster y Warwick. Doctorado en Manchester, Inglaterra. Es catedrático en la Universidad Metropolitana de Manchester, donde vive desde 1987. Es autor de* Experto en Soledades *(1978);* A la caza del eterno ciervo *(1983);* Temporal de Ausencias *(1985);* Velero de humo abandona el reino *(1993);* Oficios de Trovador *(Perú, 2006);* Las flores de tu boca *(2009);* Cuaderno del Fauno *(2017);* Pícaro Monje; Mal de no verte; Poemas sobre el Atlántico *(e-books-2018) y* Obra Reunida *(UNJBG-2018).*

Interjección

Otra subida: "Avancen al fondo".
Otro microbús: Línea 73
Otro asiento: Ventana.
Un empujón: Mueca.
Otra chica: Glúteos.
Otro policía: Silbato.
Otra mirada: Neurótico.
Un recuerdo: Ángel.
Otro recuerdo: Teresa.
Otro empujón: Carajo.

Padre

Obrero de
los caminos.
Ante ti
me inclino,
y
no tengo sombrero, como tú,
para
quitármelo.

(De: Experto en soledades)

Interjection

Again onboard: "Move towards the back".
Another bus; Bus 73
Another seat: Window.
Someone pushing: A smirk.
Another girl: Buttocks.
Another policeman: Whistle.
Another glance: Neurotic.
A memory: Angel.
Another memory: Teresa.
Someone else pushing: Damn.

Father

A labourer
along roadways.
Before you
I bow
and,
unlike you, I have no hat
to remove.

(From: Experto en soledades)

Urbanidad

Si por mi fuera:
En este mismo momento

Pero,
¿No crees que debemos guardar
cierto decoro en los tranvías?

Orfandad

Nuevamente me atraen
los parques solitarios
y otra vez
en las hojas de álamos tristes
he visto desde mi soledad
navajas a la medida de mi nostalgia

Barnizando el pecho de lágrimas
aguardando estoy la lluvia

Todavía permanecen a mi lado
el jazmín sangriento
esa alegría aún no cantada
mi infancia
aquella huérfana
de este viejo tambor

(De: A la caza del eterno ciervo)

Civility

If I had my way:
In this exact moment

But,
Don't you think
we need to behave
with certain decorum onboard a bus?

Orphanhood

Once again, I am drawn
to solitary parks
and again,
looking up from my solitude,
on the leaves of gloomiest elms
I have seen
blades that were custom-made for
my yearning

Tears varnishing my chest
I wait for the rain

Still by my side
a jasmine tinted with blood
that kind of joy still to be sung
my childhood
nothing but an orphan
of this old drummer

(From: A la caza del eterno ciervo)

Abrígame con tus ojos

A mi tío, don Enrique Paucar Machaca

Hombre una y tantas veces
como sea necesario

Abrígame con tus ojos
como el musgo abriga la fría piedra
háblame de la muerte llena de luz
esparciendo sus pasos
tus manos brotando de mi pecho
olvidado tantas veces sobre el óxido de la ciudad
estruendo de sol sobre los campos

Aguárdame tras el primer atisbo de lluvia
no llores
esta vez
cobijaré tus manos
no dejaré que el hosco viento y la nevada
marchiten tus sueños
hombre una y tantas veces cierto
entre estos cansancios
entre estos yantares

Acércate y toma de mi vaso
que ahora mudo y desordenado
registra tu ausencia
ahora que irremediablemente se acerca
la noche en esta habitación
donde sólo van quedando el jazz y tus manos
la sombra dulce formada por tus ojos cerrados

Shelter me with your eyes

To my uncle, don Enrique Paucar Machaca

Man, once and as many times as
may be necessary

Shelter me with your eyes
like moss sheltering the cold stone
and talk to me about a death so full of light
scattering its steps,
your hands sprouting from my chest
so many times forgotten above the rust of the city
the roar of the sun over fields

Wait for me after the first inkling of rain
do not cry
this time
I shall shield your hands
and not allow the rough wind and the snow
to wither your dreams
Man, once true and many times true,
amid this tiredness
amid these repasts

Come close and take my cup,
this speechless and haphazard cup
at present recording your absence
now that night itself inexorably encroaches on this
room
and what remains is solely jazz, your hands,
the sweet shadow fashioned by your eyes closing

entreabriendo levemente mi memoria
tus manos acercándome la lluvia
registrando la húmeda transparencia
el sol por las mañanas
Hombre una y tantas veces
entre la triste batalla de la garúa
he convocado a este silencio
sin llamarte

Ya no acudes al llanto
como otras veces
al desamparo
morsa tristemente olvidada
sobre los campos de asfalto y de lluvia
por última vez escucha esta canción
lo único verdaderamente mío
que hoy puedo acercar a tus labios

(De: Temporal de ausencias)

El asombro del fuego

Es difícil huir de este milagro
De este viejo asombro que perpleja la mente
Ahora, que entre el verdor
De esta isla fría y lejana,
El recuerdo del primer fulgor de mi infancia,
Allá en el duro desierto de Tacna,
Se quema en la desdicha y en la congoja.

quietly leaving my memories ajar
your hands bringing the rain closer
recording its humidity and transparency
and the morning sun
Man, once and so many times,
amid the miserable battle brought on by this drizzle
I have summoned silence
without calling out to you

You no longer resort to weeping
as you did before
or to helplessness
like some sadly forgotten seahorse
on fields of asphalt and rain,
and so do listen to this song one last time,
it is the only thing truly mine
that today I can bring closer
to your lips

(From: Temporal de ausencias)

Bewildering fire

How hard it is to get away from this marvel, away
From this ancient wonder that baffles the mind
Now that, amongst the foliage in this cold, far away island,
The memory of the first glow of my childhood,
back in the harsh desert of Tacna,
burns within the embers of misery and grief.

Aquí, en el equivocado lado de Itaca,
Frente a la victoriana chimenea
Fino es el brillo y el destello
Que hacen tolerable y pasadero
Este opaco y cruel inverno.

Pero en la misma llama que cruje en el madero,
Mismo el asombro y la música que fosforea
Que espejea en los ojos del niño y
Que ahora ilumina la memoria del seco paisaje
Allá en la otra fogata del distante hemisferio

Misma es también la sorpresa
Que alegra, que fluye
Que se hilvana en el corazón
Y en el leve unicornio
Que se desvanece en el luminoso sueño

Sé que como ésta
Y otras veces volveré a celebrar
(con Borges, tal vez)
La milenaria lumbre;
Ese antiguo y secreto misterio,
Este viejo y nuevo don de cada día
Que ningún ser humano
puede mirar sin un asombro antiguo.

And so here, on the wrong side of Ithaca,
facing that Victorian fireplace,
such fine gleam and glisten
make this cruel, opaque winter
at least tolerable, endurable.

But within the flames creaking in the burning wood
that same astoundment, that same music
sparkling bright,
glinting in the eyes of a child and
now lighting up the memory of the driest landscape from far away,
at that other bonfire
in a distant hemisphere

Moreover, it is the same surprise
that elates us, that runs in streams,
that attaches itself in stitches to the heart,
and it is also that same nimble unicorn
fading into shimmering sleep

I know I will once again rejoice,
In the same way I now rejoice and have done
at other times
(alongside Borges, maybe)
This thousand-year-old blaze;
An ancient, secret mystery,
A daily gift, an offering both new and deeply-rooted,
For no human being can gaze at fire without
beholding it
in age-old wonderment

Regreso al reino

Un hombre orina la simiente de un árbol
en la Avenida Abancay mira al desconocido
las palabras
       los espejos saliendo de sus manos
un poco de muerte oscureciendo los linderos

El arribado de nuevo al reino avanza
trata de compilar el llanto de los pájaros
corazón y rostro azogados por el cansancio
asienten
     intentan en vano humedecer
modelar el espanto
        la brusca desazón

Una mosca ensaya labrada simetría
se traslada
     e instala definitiva
en la voz que sobrevive al swing
bloqueando
     aleteo de jazz en la tarde

Delgadas plantas entre el reciente smog
únicas zonas de posible canción
anuncian como una romanza de vencidos
la llegada
     el regreso al reino

Ahora es difícil hallar el presente
vuelve a doler este pozo de la dicha
donde se marcharon para siempre
las colinas
     y con ellas la humedad

(De: Oficios de trovador)

Returning to the kingdom

A man pees the seed of a tree
in Abancay Avenue, looking into the unknown
words
      mirrors leaving his hands
a little piece of death darkening adjacent lands

He who once again arrived in the kingdom
tries to amass the weeping of birds
his heart and face silvered by tiredness
nodding in agreement
     in vain trying to moisten
and shape the dread that is felt,
       that abrupt disquiet

A fly's attempts at thorough symmetry
it moves
    and settles decisively
on a voice surviving swing
blocking
     the flutter of jazz in the afternoon

Slender plants reveal themselves through the recent smog,
the only sites for a possible song
announcing, like a ballad of the defeated,
the arrival
     the return to the kingdom

It is now difficult to unearth the present time
this well of bliss is aching once again
where the hills left forever
     taking their moistness away

(From: Oficios de trovador)

Quijote en Manchester

por el victoriano canal camina
imaginando los campos de alhucema,
el caliente, efervescente vaho,
la gigante polvareda en el errante camino,
la templada nobleza de La Mancha.

quijada vencida a estos malos vientos,
cansado, rendido y seco,
aprieta la adarga, la tenue voluntad de vivir
que aún sobreviven en la mente hidalga.

sin molinos que lo aturdan
cruzando los filos del profundo invierno,
coteja los últimos claros de la tarde,
los desvelos, las crueldades del amor;
memoriza unos cuantos nombres propios,
frescas lágrimas lavan,
lamen el oxidado peto.

sabe que soñar es su destino
y escribir la sincopada pena, su condena;
en la ruma de libros no leídos,
mentalmente acomoda una a una
gastadas metáforas, amuletos, monedas,
trinos, trovas que envejecen
en castillos de hueso y polvo.

por un breve momento cree cabalgar
por las verdes colinas de la ajena patria que le cobija

Don Quixote in Manchester

along the Victorian waterway he walks
imagining fields of lavandula,
the hot and effervescent mist,
the gigantic cloud of dust along the wandering route,
the bold nobility of La Mancha.

his jawbone giving in to these tough winds,
tired, weary, dried-up,
he holds on tightly to his leather shield, his faint
desire to live,
all of it surviving in his noble mind.

without windmills to daze him,
crossing the edges of deepest winter
he cross-checks the last lights of the afternoon,
the sleeplessness, the cruelties of love;
he memorises a few proper nouns,
fresh tears will wash and lick
the rusty breastplate.

he knows well that dreaming is his destiny
and that writing down his syncopated grief is
his condemnation;
in that heap of unread books,
he mentally accommodates, one by one,
tattered metaphors, amulets, coins,
trills, verses that grow old
in castles made from bone and dust.

y parece existir en la dulce dicha que le ofrecen
el lenguaje y la música de Inglaterra;
pero vacila y lo abate la interminable lluvia,
la desesperanza, la congoja que agrieta otra vez
los suburbios del desconsuelo,
rasgando las esquinas, los rescoldos del alma,
haciendo más urgente la distante copla,
las guitarras, la melodía y el materno signo:
el guerrero castizo sonido de Castilla.

está solo y tiene miedo
pues sabe que el valor
es también un don escaso
que los avaros dioses demandan y prestan;
y sabiendo lejano el mar,
se resigna a no llorar.

dolor en bandolera, como puede,
armado de viejas, heroicas hombrías
queja a queja, verso a verso,
despacio, avanza:
celebra el asombro y la belleza de la noche,
en la furia de la primera helada del año:
humilde y loco, cree balbucear una línea,
desnudo, renace y se redime en la palabra,
la mínima, la indecible;
asustado, resiste el afilado viento,
compendia la sublime gloria de la derrota:
los altos, espléndidos,
magníficos fracasos de su vida.

(De: Las flores de tu boca)

for a brief moment, he thinks he is riding
over the green fields of a foreign motherland that
gives him shelter
and seemingly he exists in the sweet delight that England's
music and language proffer;
but he dithers, downcast as he is by that unrelenting rain,
despair, anguish that opens cracks once again
along the outskirts of his grief,
tearing at the corners, the cinders of his soul,
calling out the urgency of that remote refrain,
with its guitars and its melodies and the maternal sign of the zodiac:
the echoes of Castile: born and bred, warrior-like.

he is alone and afraid
for he knows that any courage that may be had
is also a rare gift
which miserly gods demand and give on loan;
and knowing that the sea is far away,
he yields to shedding no tears.

such pain strapped to him, as well as it can be,
armed as he is with that old and heroic manliness,
and grievance by grievance, verse by verse,
slowly he proceeds
celebrating the marvel and beauty of the night,
amid the furious first frost that year:
for he is both meek and mad, and believes he is
stammering a line of text,
naked as he is, he feels reborn finding redemption in words,
even in the least important words, even in unsayable words;
yet he is now scared as he withstands the sharp-edged wind,
as he summarises the sublime glory of defeat:

Reclamo del poeta y buen amante

Si solo fui para ti el amante iletrado,
comedido y puntual ejecutor
del indecente y gustoso mete
y
saca
audaz y atento proveedor
del pélvico empuje,
del acompasado y duro follar
que muele tus adentros;
es decir, si solo fui tu buen fornicador,
no más, no menos.

entonces,
me podrías decir:
¿quién fue el que
—en una noche sin luna—
al verte venir a mí
escribió en la arena
que lucirías aún más hermosa
si en este momento
la lluvia de estrellas cayera sobre ti?

(De: Cuaderno del fauno)

all those deep, splendid
and magnificent failures in his life.

(From: Las flores de tu boca)

A call to the poet and to the good lover

If I was only an illiterate lover for you,
an understated and precise performer
regarding the indecent and delectable *in*
and
out
a bold and thoughtful provider
of pelvic thrusts,
of the rhythmic and hard fucking
that grinds your insides;
that is to say, if I was only a good fornicator
for you, no more and no less than that.

then,
can you tell me:
who was the man
—on that moonless night—
who, when seeing you coming towards me,
wrote on the sand
that you would appear as an even more
beautiful woman
if, at that precise moment,
stars rained over you?

(From: Cuaderno del fauno)

LUIS REBAZA SORALUZ
(Perú)

Luis Rebaza Soraluz has worked in multiple disciplines since 1978: poetry, fiction, Arts, Cultural History, Visual Arts, and the Latin American *Fin de Siècle*. He currently holds a professorship at King's College London. He has published poetry, short stories and cultural research studies; has worked on illustrations and graphic design; and has edited and published bilingual hand-made chapbooks under the imprint La Yapa Editores. In 2005 a selection of his literary work was included in the Mexican anthologies *Caudal de piedra: veinte poetas peruanos (1955-1971)* and *Estática doméstica: Tres generaciones de cuentistas peruanos (1951-1981)*, both published by *Universidad Nacional Autónoma de México (UNAM)*.

Luis Rebaza Soraluz ha trabajado interdisciplinariamente desde 1978 en las áreas de poesía, narrativa, las artes, la historia cultural, la visualidad y también el Fin de Siècle hispanoamericano. Es actualmente profesor del King's College London. Ha publicado poesía, relato e investigación cultural; hecho ilustración y diseño gráfico; y sido el editor de plaquetas bilingües hechas a mano y publicadas bajo el sello de La Yapa Editores. En 2005 una selección de su obra literaria fue incluida en las antologías mexicanas Caudal de piedra: veinte poetas peruanos *(1955-1971) y* Estática doméstica: Tres generaciones de cuentistas peruanos *(1951-1981), publicadas por la UNAM.*

Las llaves

Quien consigue las llaves
no posee la puerta
Es dueño de una fórmula
De un soplo

Y a quien el acero
le fragua las manos
en verdad desconoce
su peso

Por más que las arroje
al jardín de la noche
Y exista testimonio
O yazga un cuerpo

Otro sexo es una llave
Un ojo de la aguja
Un espiral carnado
La aldaba de otro pecho

Quien obtiene las llaves
no ha hollado el lindel
Es señor sin terreno
Es un ala del pacto

Y quien ciña un manojo
en su coraza
No ha defendido el paso
No ha penetrado huerto

The keys

Those who get hold of the keys
do not own the door
They own a formula
They own breath itself

And those whose hands
are forged by iron
are truly unaware of
their weight

No matter how often they may be plunged
into the gardens of the night
and however many witnesses
or however obvious a body lying there for all to see

Another sex is a key
The eye of the needle
A red spiral
the hasp on someone else's chest

Those who get hold of the keys
have not stomped on the lintel of the door
Lords they are without lands
Having signed a single-sided pact

And those who squeeze a bunch of keys
against their breastplate
Have not defended the crossing
Have not infiltrated the orchard

La epopeya es un reino
en la puerta
que no palpan
las manos

Y recorre el jardín
con las manos quemadas
quien siempre transita
la puerta que no tiene

Ah demos el paso
que devele
qué se lleva
Su lado oculto

Llevados en las llaves

Por un ancla en el cuerpo

Epics are kingdoms in themselves
within the door
yet untouched
by hands

And those who keep crossing the door
they do not own
will walk along the gardens
with burnt hands

Ah, so let's take the plunge
to unveil
what its hidden side
drags away

Within the keys,

Within an anchor, within the body

Hotel Portofino 1981

Nadar entre la espuma de los choros y el panal de jabón
o rodar en el piso
lejos de una ducha salada que pudiera contener
dos vasos de licor y en el hielo una grabación de nuestras
propias voces
curvados en la amistad y persiguiendo los sonidos
que señalaban el zaguán y el rellano de los pisos:
una morena caliente paseando sobre su piel
quemada y abrazada quién sabe cuántas veces
sin la mínima ampolladura
También enfrentar al sol
silbar como el pez al gorrión equivocado y equivocando
la ambición con el gabinete de ropa de cama de los huéspedes
preguntar quién quitó a quién o quién en quién
busca una persona que se hunde en el amor a cada salto
y en la espalda del siguiente se deshace.

Nadie evade proseguir el soliloquio porque también estaban allí los peces
en su vejiga flotante como el hotel donde un hombre se registra
y apacigua su sueño
o busca solitariamente un excusado
Dime qué fue de la morena que zigzagueaba su cintura
como el apuro de un escote confuso
y enredado en el cabello de la ropa que se quita
una mujer de amarillo o una mujer morena
cómo sería lo sentido o por sentir
en esa mujer sola o en las dos juntas
o en una convirtiéndose en la otra porque
lo cierto es que entró una mujer morena y salió una mujer de amarillo
como si el cuarto doscientosdiecisiete fuera

Hotel Portofino 1981

Swimming along the foam of mussels and a soapy hive
or rolling on the floor
away from the brackish shower that might contain
a couple of glasses of liqueur, and on the ice a recording of our
own voices
bent on our friendship, pursuing sounds that
pointed at the hallway and the landing between floors:
a dark warm woman strolling, her skin burnt
and embraced who knows how many
times, without a single blister
Confronting the sun too,
whistling like a fish would whistle to the sparrow that was both
confused and confusing
any ambitions one may have
apropos the wardrobe with bedclothes for any guests
who may show up
and then asking who took what from whom or who
looks in whom for someone who sinks in love after every leap
they take and then dissolves into the back
of the next person.

No one avoids continuing with their soliloquy
because fish were also there, their bladders floating just like the hotel
                                    [where a man books a room
to appease his sleep
or looks all on his own for a restroom
Tell me what happened to that dark-haired woman whose waist zigzagged
much like the trouble caused by her fuzzy décolletage
entangled with her hair over the clothes she removes,
is it a woman dressed in yellow or a dark-haired woman

un portal convertido en ventana
donde se oye el mar desde un laberíntico oído
que admirara la calle como admiramos nuestra
propia infidelidad
infinitamente desdichados
porque son cuatro cojudos en un mismo
mortero los cuatro sueñan ser el tiempo
pero el tiempo en palabras que se alzan
de madrugada y de madrugada también
se acuestan y nadan y albergan una mano de
mujer donde más viriles son
abarca la desilusión y el atragantamiento.

Sólo sentarse en un pueblo pequeño y dedicarse a la hartura de dirigirse la palabra
recuerdas Pisco fue antes de Pisco después de Pisco
resbalaba por el mar era dorado o sediento como el vientre
de un pez en la media noche
atravesaba la arena segado por azules ojos
fue un sueño lo que hizo de San Andrés el cuerpo
de un niño flotando entre las olas
o fue una fuente qué pensaría de los senos casi descubiertos
y el vientre que se muestra ennegrecido y público entre los bañistas
O fue una suerte de filo de mar como el lomo de un pez
o el aroma intenso de un verano echado sobre un vaso
un plato de pescado cortado y zumado en limón
y ese lazo de nuestro sueño multiplicado en cuatro
donde velas son obscenidades y lanchas cortando el mar
azul en el rojo horizonte nos recuerdan lo pubianos
que terminan todos los pensamientos.

Porque todos bebimos la inmensidad
y vimos jinetes dividiendo las olas con sus rojas espadas

what would one feel now or later
with only one of the two, or possibly with
both of them,
or perhaps with one becoming the other because
the truth is that a dark-haired woman entered and
the one who left
was a woman dressed in yellow
as if room twohundredandseventeen stood as a
doorway that turned into a window
from which you were able to hear the sea with a
labyrinthine ear admiring
the street as we admire our own
infidelity
infinitely wretched as we feel
because they are but four jerks in the same
pestle, all four dreaming about being time itself
but the type of time that manifests in words arising at dawn,
and once again at dawn go back
to sleep and swim and clasp a woman's
hand at their most virile
encompassing
disappointment and gagging.

Do you remember just sitting there in a small town and what it was to speak to this one
and that one until you had had enough, do you remember Pisco as it was
before Pisco and as it will be after Pisco,
and sliding along the sea it was either golden or thirsty like the
belly of a fish at midnight
crossing the sands severed by blue eyes,
it was a dream that changed the harbour at San Andrés
into the body of a child floating among the waves
or possibly a fountain, so what would have been

hacia el apocalipsis dirigían las olas como el pastor
que lleva seguro su rebaño
Nosotros lo vimos
ya cerca del mar y con el borrado recuerdo
de delfines desollados junto a las barcas
multiplicadas por cada conchilla o caracola
reseca y brillante pulida entre las otras con su roce
En la arena no eran más que esa soledad imperfecta
o esa multiplicación que convierte a cada una en un
torpe seguro de su consistencia contra otras
y en donde lentamente perfecciona su cuerpo
y se destruye golpeada la una contra la otra
y mezclada entre la arena o aun
como la mala semilla
cayendo entre los yuyos
conservarse intacta
O al llegar a un hotel de la pequeña población de Pisco
ser pisada por un personaje que abre la puerta 217 y escucha
ese sonido y palpa el polvo como figura aquí
esa ósea protección
que sólo se transforma
en un viaje que hicimos nosotros y alguno
recuerda real cuando está solo el eco de su voz
esa maravilla que quisimos vivir
y en donde nos perdimos uno a uno
resbalando entre la espuma de los choros y el panal de jabón
golpeados los unos con los otros
en el hirviente cristal
hasta producir aquella chispa.

2 de enero de 1981
Amistad para Kike, Carlos, Edgar.

made of almost bare breasts or a blackened belly
seen publicly among bathers
Or it was a type of blade from the sea like the loin of a fish
or the intense aroma of a summer tossed into a glass
a plate of fish, cut up in pieces and sprinkled with the juice of a lemon,
and the tether of our dream times four
where sails are obscenities and barges clipping
the blue sea on the red horizon remind us
how pubic all thoughts end up being.

Because we all drank from that vastness
and we saw horsemen splitting the waves with their red swords
and guiding them towards the Apocalypse itself
just like shepherds safely steer their flock
We saw it
so close to the sea, with a faded memory
of skinned dolphins close to the boats
swollen by all those shells or conchs
parched and gleaming, buffed to a shine by
brushing against others
And on the sand, they were no more than imperfect solitude or the kind of
multiplication that turns each one into an awkward assurance of their consistency
as opposed to others
and where it slowly perfects its shape
and is destroyed, one pounding against another,
and blending with the sand or even as
the bad seed
sinking among seaweed
and remaining intact
Or when arriving at the hotel in the small town of Pisco
to be stepped upon by a character
who opens door 217 and listens

El lago

Cuando llegamos
adiviné el lago.
Adiviné su centro como quien posa
un pie de noche en una isla.
Y vi que lo perdía conforme se doraba
el color del agua en lo lejano.
Y hallé otro centro en el remolino.
A donde pude llegar.
Conquistado en la fiebre.

Y luego playas y ella no
que descansaba.
Tanto orillas afuera como dentro
unidas por un acuático suelo.
Nunca pisado, rozado apenas
por aletas inseguras, por ojos verdes.

Y así como llegué en la noche
así he partido.
Así olvido.
Así deshago mi adivinanza
y quedan signos que se desvanecen.
Algo que se abre y algo
que ahora se cierra cuando paso.
Busco un viejo camino
en el agua.

para Stephanie
2 de marzo de 1983

to that sound and feels the dust as it is here,
that bone-like protection
that is only transformed
into a journey that we embarked upon and which someone remembers as real
when the only thing there
is the echo
of their voice
that marvel that we wished to experience
and where we became lost one by one
as we skidded between the foam of mussels and the soapy hive
battering against each other
in the scalding glass
until they yielded that spark.

2 January 1981
In friendship for Kike, Carlos, Edgar.

The lake

When we arrived,
I had foreseen there was to be a lake.
I had rightly guessed what would be in its very centre
like someone who sets foot at night on an island.
And I saw that I was letting it slip as the water turned gold in the distance.
And I found another midpoint in that whirlpool.
I was able to reach it.
Vanquished by my fever.

And then it was about beaches, but not her,

Ventana que no es

Ahora podías perfectamente
mostrarme tu vida por la ventana
como unos cuadros que nadie ha pintado
José Coronel Urtecho

Dices que en veinte años
vas a atravesar un territorio
como la piel de un tambor.
Qué irás a decir
de tu silencio,
de tu piel de ladrillo y
el miedo de tus camas.
Se agotan tus ojos y
se agota la luz de tus pisadas.

Y hoy día buscas una llave
bajo esta puerta abierta
buscas una llave.

La boca como un tambor,
tus brazos delgados como un tambor,
el fondo de la selva como un tambor,
también la edad que marea tu cuerpo
redobla y se estira al borde
de un tambor. Y
como un tambor
llegas a un idioma que jamás
has tocado,
no hay lágrimas, no hay sorpresas.
Porque tu mano guía

she was just resting.
There were shores both outside and inside,
linked by an aquatic base.
Never once stepped upon, barely skimmed
by hesitant fins and green eyes.

And in the same way I arrived at night,
I left the place.
That is how to forget, and
how I unravel my riddle,
and any signs that may remain will fade too.
Something opens up and, when I pass alongside it,
something closes.
And I am searching for that old trail
on the water.

for Stephanie
2 March 1983

A window that is not

Now you could perfectly
show me what your life has been through a window,
just like a series of paintings that
no one had ever painted
José Coronel Urtecho

What you are saying is that in twenty years
you will be crossing a land that
resembles the skin of a drum.
What will you then say
about your silence,

el orden de los cuerpos.
Y dónde está esa palabra fuerte
en la pared.
Dónde tus veinte años,
dónde esa ventana
y el joven de esta nave que
agita la niebla,
que embastece tus cuadros,
tus cobres, tus magnesios.
Y qué dices hoy día que
estás fuera,
grabado en este mar.
Y tus ojos cabalgan hacia el marco,
la piel de tu tambor,
tus dos decenas,
la venda de tus ojos
que nadie ha mirado

Epílogo

In memoriam Nelson Arrunátegui

Infidelidad
del dactilar intonso
del pan que no se vende
del cangrejo que avanza
con gozo

or about your brick-like skin and
the fears sprouting in your many beds.
Your eyes dry up and
any light coming from your steps is spent.
And today you are looking for a key
and even under that open door
you are still looking for a key.

Like a drum, your mouth,
your thin arms like a drum,
the depths of the rainforest like a drum,
and the aging that pesters your body
rolls and stretches on the edge of
a drum. And
like a drum
you stretch out to a language that you have never
played,
there are no tears, there are no surprises.
And this is because your hand guides
the sequence of bodies. And you ask
where is that
exacting word appearing on the wall.
Where are you aged twenty,
where is the window
and the young man on board a vessel
jolted by the fog,
the one who replenishes
your paintings,
your brass, the magnesium ribbon for your photographs.
And what can you say now that
you are away,
engraved on this stretch of sea.

del impar monociclo

   Fidelidad
del iris del cerrojo del marinero cuyas miles
de amadas
naufragan

   Infidelidad
del espejo sin plata
del fruto verde y caído
del fruto maduro y en el árbol
siempre

   Fidelidad
del único que espera
del último que sale
del que reina aguja entre
alfileres
ciegos

   Perfección
del impúber
del eunuco
del unicelular
del soltero que hierve
la olla sin
el agua

   Infidelidad
que conduce su animal al baño

And your eyes ride towards the frame,
the skin of your drum,
your two times ten,
the blindfold over your eyes
that no one has looked at.

Epilogue

To Nelson Arrunátegui,
In memoriam

    The unfaithfulness
of an unshorn fingerprint
of bread that will not sell
of the crab that proceeds
with elation

    The faithfulness
of the eye within its keyhole
of an uneven unicycle
of the sailor whose thousands
of lovers
were all shipwrecked

    The unfaithfulness
of the mirror without a silver backing
of the fallen, green fruit
of the ripe fruit always on the tree

    The faithfulness

Fidelidad
que da ser a la tregua abriendo fuego

Son llaves
son noches
son cuerpos

of the only one who awaits
of the last one to leave
of those reigning as a needle
reigns among blind
pins

    Perfection
of the prepubescent
of the eunuch
of the unicellular
of the single man boiling
a pan
with no water

    Unfaithfulness
driving an animal towards the bathroom

    Faithfulness
opening fire and thus giving meaning to a truce

They are but keys
they are but nights
they are but bodies

ANA MARÍA REYES BARRIOS
(Venezuela)

Ana María Reyes Barrios was born in the 1980s in Venezuela, and currently lives and works in London. She studied Art and Documentary Film, and at present she is an independent film producer. She has produced and directed several documentaries in Cuba, Venezuela, Spain and United Kingdom. She is very much a nomad in spirit, and she has travelled to a number of countries and lived in several cities throughout the world. As an author, she writes both poetry and fiction. She regularly takes part in poetry readings and literary gatherings in London, and she has co-directed the workshop *Poesía Pandémica*. Her first book, *Sombras de la sal,* was published by **equidistancias** in 2021.

Ana María Reyes Barrios nació en los años 80 en Venezuela y actualmente vive y trabaja en Londres. Estudió Arte y Cine Documental, en cuyo campo se desempeña como realizadora cinematográfica independiente. Ha producido y dirigido diversos proyectos documentales en Cuba, Venezuela, España y Reino Unido. De espíritu nómade, ha viajado por numerosas geografías y residido en diversas ciudades en el mundo. En su faceta de escritora practica la narrativa y la poesía. Participa habitualmente en lecturas y tertulias poéticas londinenses y ha codirigido el taller Poesía Pandémica.
Su primer libro, Sombras de la sal, *fue publicado en 2021 por* **equidistancias**.

Piernas terrestres

Entre las piernas lleva un silencio
de alas rojas

la cavidad dolida

la visión seca

El hueso triangular
de esquinas parcas
de guerra triste

El cuerpo memorioso
aqueja con silbidos
el usurpar lento
de araña negra
                    naciente

Brazos extendidos
que salivan los poros
regados de vacío
caídos de sombras
llenos de delirios
Las piernas pronuncian
estrategias movibles
fragilidades cínicas
itinerarios precavidos

Las piernas sofocan
el deseo y el olvido
la trampa

Land-based legs

She carries between her legs
a red-winged silence

an aching cavity

and her visions have dried-up

That triangular bone
with slender bends
waged such a sad war

The body is good at remembering
afflicted by a whistling sound
gradually snatching
a black spider
                        being born

Stretched out arms
their pores salivating
watered into emptiness
plunged from the shadows
filled with delusion
Her legs deliver
fickle strategies
such cynical fragilities
such cautious itineraries

Her legs stifle
both desire and oblivion
the snare

la lúcida trampa
de saberse vacías

Color arrebatado
por el cristal melodioso
que emite cercos de hastío
y una imagen pálida
de ave dormida

Y tiemblan las manos
resurgidas de arena
en la caída
en la fuga

en el otro:
el destierro

y se asfixia en la tierra
que trae entre las piernas

Islas magnéticas

Islas magnéticas
de sabor ascendente

Enclaves de piel tibia
de coraza terráquea
la pared del sueño
el oficio de la boca

that lucid snare
of being aware of their emptiness

All colour snatched
by such melodious glass
emitting loops of weariness
and the pale image
of a sleeping bird

And her hands tremble
resurfacing from the sand
in the downfall
while trying to get away

and on the other side:
banishment

choking with the ground
that she carries between her legs

Magnetic islands

Magnetic islands
in ascending flavours

Enclaves with warm skin
of an earthy shell
the walls of dreams
such is the craft of a mouth

Las terminaciones nerviosas desbocadas, transmigradas

El árbol crece hacia dentro
las venas también

Así los cuerpos confinados
a su propia vestimenta
a sus propias carnes y huesos

Los ojos también hacia adentro
las palmas extendidas
dilatando el cuerpo
lanzándolo al frente
intentando huir hacia el espacio

Afuera hace un sol que calma los dientes
y sobre la ventana enfurece el azul más eléctrico

Afuera huele a pájaro nuevo
a tez liberada
a cielo pesado
a orilla náufraga

Afuera las plantas estallan hacia la luz
expanden sus pieles limpiamente

Oscuro aire solar
como lluvia de septiembre al despertar

Yo duermo descalza
y apelmazada en la orilla de mi cama

Nerve endings run amok, transmigrating

The tree grows inwards
as do veins

Thus, bodies are confined
to their own garments
to their own flesh and bones

Eyes are also directed inwards
the palms of the hands spread out
dilating the body
hurling it straight ahead
fleeing towards space

Outside the sun is powerful enough to soothe
your teeth
and on the window that most electric blue
becomes enraged

What you can sense outside is the smell of a new bird
or of a freed complexion
or of heavy skies
or of castaway shores

Outside, plants are bursting in the direction of the light
freshly expanding their skins

Dark air under the sun
like September rains when waking up

I sleep barefoot

gesticulo caricias secas
que redundan el encierro

Elástica mar

Huele a grito vencido
enredado, tirado en la blanca dimensión
en el tiempo ocupado de mármoles intactos

Tan cansina la luz y tan lejos de la mitad del planeta
tan insólita la búsqueda de su cuerpo, altanero
como sombra elástica, camino deshecho
finales a medio suspiro

Tan elástica la mar
su rara tentación
su temblar místico
su principio autónomo

Tan elástica la mar que hoy es una mujer y mañana es el hombre mar
tan elástica que es posible llevarla debajo de la piel
como una instancia absoluta
como una piel más
que pocos entienden
que pocos escuchan
que pocos perciben

Tan elástica la mar, el mar, los mares, las mareas y las olas que me parieron, que me
enredaron, me revolcaron, me cobijaron, me mataron y me

matted on the edge of my bed
I mime terse caresses
bringing about this confinement

Elastic sea

The scent is that of a crushed scream
entangled and flung into that white dimension
of time contained within marble as yet unspoilt

So tiresome the light, so far away from
the other half of the planet
such an uncommon search for a proud body
like an elastic shadow, the unravelled path,
endings that are so close by

So elastic is the sea
its rare allure
its mystical shudder
its sovereign beginnings

So elastic is the sea that today it appears as a woman and
tomorrow as a man
so elastic that you can carry it under your skin
like a limitless urging
or like a second skin
that few can understand
that few can hear
that few can discern

So elastic the sea, the sea, the seas, the tides and the waves that

enterraron

Que entre sus sales me dieron hijos e hijas
lunas y soles y una montaña subacuática para esconderme y así no tener más miedo

La mar, de cuerpo salvaje en donde sobrevivirá mi piel, mi cuerpo, mi también elástico
cuerpo con su confluencia tardía

La mar había. La mar quedaba en un país que se llamaba "dondeyonací"

Trapecista elemental

Extiendo mi existencia
de golpe
como un trapecista elemental
de abajo hacia arriba
de arriba hacia abajo
sobre la superficie
limpia de reflejos

invisibles

Este papel mojado
se deja empapar de frío
palidecido

gave birth to me, that ensnared me, that
knocked me down, that sheltered me, that killed me
and buried me

So elastic the sea that its brine gave me
sons and daughters
moons and suns and a sunken mountain for me to hide
and fear no more

The sea, a wild mass where my skin and my body will survive,
yes, my also elastic body
at this belated juncture

There was a sea. It was to be found in a country
called "whereIwasborn".

Effortless trapeze artist

I abruptly outspread
my existence
like a trapeze artist performing basic moves
bottom-up
top to bottom
on the surface
there are no visible

reflections

This wet piece of paper
allows itself to be drenched with cold

traspapelado
y flota en la humedad llana
entre las manos de otros
dormidos
soñando
reclamando territorios librados
firmes azules y blancos
episodios blandos
y diluvios

un deshacerse en el silencio

Navego en el papel que he hecho barco
en la misma tina llena de otros

Y pinto caritas firmes
manos saludando al vacío
hacia las ventanitas distantes de otros
dibujadas con bolígrafos rotos
gastados de garabatos
de expresiones imaginarias
risas repentinas

Notas imprecisas
a la luz de una ventana más bien oscura

turning pale
and misplaced
floating on the flat dampness
between the hands of others
who are asleep
dreaming and
claiming emancipated lands
unwavering in blue and white
what mellow episodes
and deluges

a silent disposal

And I sail on that piece of paper that I have turned
into a boat
in that same tub, so full of others

And I draw firm little faces
hands saluting emptiness
towards those tiny and far away windows belonging to others
sketched with broken biros
worn out after so much scrawling
with imaginary expressions
and sudden laughter

Vague notes are written down
by the light of a window that is
more like darkness

XAVIERA RINGELING
(Chile)

Xaviera Ringeling was born in Paraguay and is a Chilean national. She is currently based in London. She has a degree in Philosophy from Pontificia Universidad Católica in Chile, and she completed an MS in Environmental Studies at UCL. She founded the poetry group "Poesía Pandémica", and she plays an active part in the Greenwich Poetry Workshop. Her poetry collection *La oblicua luz de la tarde* was awarded the *XXXII Premio Voces Nuevas* by the Spanish publisher Torremozas, and was included in an anthology by this publisher, as well as in the anthology *Leyendo Poesía in London*. Her other poetry collection, *Alba*, was published in London by El Ojo de la Cultura in 2019.

Xaviera Ringeling, de nacionalidad chilena, nació en Paraguay y actualmente está radicada en Londres. Estudió filosofía en la Pontificia Universidad Católica de Chile y posteriormente completó un magister en medioambiente en UCL. Precursora del colectivo poético "Poesía Pandémica", Xaviera también participa activamente del taller Greenwich Poetry Workshop. Su poemario La oblicua luz de la tarde *fue galardonado con el XXXII Premio Voces Nuevas de la editorial española Torremozas, e incluido en una antología realizada por la misma editorial, y luego en la antología* Leyendo Poesía in London. *Ha publicado además un libro individual de poemas,* Alba *(El Ojo de la Cultura, Londres 2019).*

Distancias

asirme a tu piel

para combatir insomnios
anclados en el nervio ocular batido

para aplacar en tu calor
mi anochecer de crecientes palpitaciones

y la distancia entre el plexo solar sintiente

y todas las pieles amadas

Londres

tu masa gris
deviene aeropuerto continuo
           del azul

deviene escalera mecánica
circular

Distances

I hold on to your skin

to fight insomnia
anchored on an overpowered optic nerve

to subdue in your warmth
my nightfall of growing palpitations

and the distance between the feeling solar plexus

and those skins beloved

London

your grey mass
turns continuous airstrip
          of the blue

turns automated circular
escalator

Mañana

en el desvarío de mirar todas las ventanas hasta
                                        Cannon Street

y de bailar con las sombras en cada cuarto
                                                solitario

cada historia   cada carencia y secreto placer
                                        contra el vidrio

 cada vida reflejada en la propia
                    hasta que el tren divida el Támesis

hasta que el flujo que nos une   nos separe   hasta

                                                Mañana

En terreno ajeno

reina la carencia de sueño y la infalible torpeza:
ilimitada capacidad para el error

que nos mantiene la carne delgada
permeable sobre los huesos

y hay doscientas tragedias
para humedecer días soleados
hay un dolor distante-presente
un aluvión sempiterno en el lugar

Morning

delirious   looking at every window all the way to
                                    Cannon Street

dancing with shadows   inhabiting every solitary
                                    room

every story   every deprivation every secret pleasure
                                    against the windowpane

each life reflected in our own
                    until the train splits the Thames in two

until the flow that unites us   divides us   until

                                    Tomorrow

In alien land

lack of sleep and steadfast clumsiness prevail:
unlimited capacity to fail

that keeps our flesh lean
permeable upon the bone

for there are two-hundred tragedies
soaking sunny days
this distant yet present affliction
an unrelenting flood where

donde habita la palabra   –familia–
la pérdida se repite se renueva   allí

desde esta isla de menguantes garantías
a miles de kilómetros de distancia

suavizamos culpas con modestas transferencias
electrónicas

Esperando

mi
temperamento
se golpea
contra las
doscientas
cincuenta y tres
paredes
de otro día
contando
dígitos
esperado
el alud
allí en
la franja
entre mar
y cordillera
esa tierra
apretada

the word   –family–   breathes
loss is repeated   it renews itself   there

from this island of decreasing safeguards
thousands of kilometres away

we cushion guilt with trifling electronic
transfers

Waiting

my
temperament
bangs against
two hundred
and fifty-three
walls of yet
another day
counting digits
waiting for
an avalanche
in that strip
between sea
and mountain
that constricted
land
where
the heavy
rock

por donde
rueda
la pesada
piedra
de mi
pasado

futuros   desdibujados
sonámbulos   futuros

en el desconcierto de ir rodando

la roca a ciegas

y esos deseos de ala corta
nuestros proyectos moribundos

lo que acaece ahora
soberana

es la pregunta

tempestades de verano   subcutáneas
ininteligibles   tempestades de verano

qué quisiera yo

saber la respuesta a esta adultez
de insospechados caminos sobrepuestos

of my past
reels

blurred   futures
sleepwalking   futures

bewildered   blindly
ramming the rock upwards

and those short-winged yearnings
our perishing projects

what takes place now
supreme

is the question

summer tempests   subcutaneous
unintelligible   summer tempests

how I wish

to know the answer to this adulthood
of unsuspected   superimposed paths

of captive ideals
of endeavours that bear no seed

de ideales cautivos
de empeños carentes de semilla

Con o sin fruto

escuálido endometrio
vierte exiguas sangres

y el dolor   el insoportable
tal vez sin propósito en mí

retorna hoy la sentencia
el usado discurso del patriarca:

~~una mujer~~ sin hijos
no hay nada más triste que una mujer sin hijos

hembra yerma hembra sin ser — *para ellos*
he de ser — hembra yerma hembra sin ser

pero no sabrá mi progenie de qué luminaria
intestina he de crear yo la vida
no sabrán ellos que no tengo nombre
no sabrán que con o sin fruto
engendro la luz

De qué sirve decir adiós a esta hora

encuentros distendidos por suelos grisáceos

With or without fruit

emaciated endometrium
discharges scant blood

and the pain   the unbearable
possibly without a purpose within me

summons today the sentence
the patriarch's worn lecture:

a woman without children
there is nothing sadder than a woman without children

female barren female without being — for them
I must be — *female barren female without being*

yet my forefathers ignore from what intestinal
floodlight I will myself create life
they do not know that I have no name
they do not know that with or without fruit

I engender light

What is the point of saying goodbye at this hour

loose meetings over greyish floors

olvidados como las colillas de tus cigarrillos
en la nebulosa de tu omisión

paloma sucia de plaza –nuestra amistad–
extinguida de pronto como una plaga

de qué sirve decir adiós ahora
si mi dolor no te toca

mi mesa está puesta
                y no llega nadie a comer

Sortilegio

el retorno
a aquel
sanguíneo
sortilegio de
cavidades ocultas
y una boca
sin dientes
ni lengua
que te sigue
que se abre
que te envuelve
que te traga

forgotten like the stubs of your cigarettes
in the blur of your omissions

filthy-square-pigeon   our friendship
extinguished suddenly like a plague

what is the point of saying goodbye at this hour
if my pain does not move you

my table is set
                yet no one comes to eat

Incantation

the return
of that blood-bound
incantation
of hidden cavities
a mouth
without teeth
or tongue
that follows
that opens
that encircles
that swallows

Caemos

caemos – como dice el poeta
desde la materna hondura
sin rebote
sin eco
caemos
pedestales en trizas
y todos los personales imperios en llamas
el latido mismo es lo único que vuelve aún
desde la jaula del pecho
donde guardamos todas las aves alerta
mientras caemos
como el ancla que somos

mientras caemos

Deja el agua correr

sobre las pequeñas cumbres del agua
nacidas de la brisa de este norte multipolar:

el laborioso

no vi en el diario delirio
no vi entre el intoxicado aire de la urbe

me dejé caer al cálculo del dígito
en el lento avanzar de la rueda a la resta

We fall

we fall – as the poet says
from maternal depths
without rebound
without echo
we fall
pedestals in shatters
and all inner empires on fire
only the heartbeat itself   still returns
from the cage of our chest
where we keep all birds alert
as we fall
as the load that we are

as we fall

Let the water run

over the small pinnacles of water
born from breeze in this multipolar North:

the industrious

I did not see in the daily delirium
I did not see through the urb's intoxicated air

I let myself go into the heave of digits
in the slow pull of the wheel towards subtraction

en aquella cifra que niega la migaja y que nos devora
el pan de la vida

a la carrera por el río mirando el agua   ciega

no sé qué recuerdo indómito caballo del curso certero
me dijo me dio el inequívoco mandato:

levanta la vista del agua sucia del paso de los días

mortal que dueles

lo tienes todo ya y del todo eres en la luz
que se bifurca

no existe la cima sino el fondo luminaria
donde destellas imperpetua como eres

y dejas de ser

y el agua   el agua sucia del Támesis
corre hacia el mar sin consecuencia

in that sum that denies the crumbs and devours
the bread of life

rushing along the river looking at the water   blind

I do not know which untamed memory   horse of unerring track
told me   gave me the unequivocal command:

lift your eyes from the dirty waters of days gone by

wounded mortal

you already have everything and you are everything
within the light that breaks

there is no summit but background   luminary
where you glow impermanent as you are

and you cease to be

and these waters   the dirty waters of the Thames
run towards the sea without consequence

GABY SAMBUCCETTI
(Argentina)

Gaby Sambuccetti was born in Argentina, in 1986, and is a UK-based writer. She holds a BA Creative Writing from Brunel University (London), she is a teacher of Latin American & Spanish Literature (Argentina), and she also holds a MA in Modern Languages, Literature and Culture from King's College London for which she was awarded with the *Von Schlippenbach* PGT bursary and later on, with the *Cosmo Davenport-Hines* poetry prize for 2022. She is the founder and director of La Ninfa Eco. Previously, she was Events Co-Director at the Oxford Writers' House (Oxford). In 2019 and 2022, she was invited to the House of Lords (UK) to be part of a discussion about writing, as well as to perform her poems as an author. Her books, reviews and contributions have appeared in a number of magazines, anthologies and literary projects in Argentina, Brazil, Peru, Germany, Bolivia, the US, Mexico, Chile, Spain, Bangladesh, India and the UK.

Gaby Sambuccetti (Argentina, 1986) es una escritora argentina radicada en el Reino Unido. Tiene una Licenciatura en Escritura Creativa de la Universidad de Brunel (Londres), es profesora de Literatura (Argentina) y también tiene una maestría en Lenguas Modernas, Literatura y Cultura de King's College London (Reino Unido) para la cual obtuvo la beca Von Schlippenbach y, posteriormente, el premio de poesía "Cosmo Davenport-Hines" edición 2022. Es fundadora y directora de la organización La Ninfa Eco. Anteriormente, fue codirectora de eventos del Oxford Writers' House (Oxford). En el 2019 y el 2022, fue invitada al Parlamento Británico para formar parte de un debate sobre escritura, así como para leer sus poemas como autora. Sus libros, reseñas y contribuciones han aparecido en varias revistas, antologías y proyectos literarios de Argentina, Brasil, Perú, Alemania, Bolivia, Estados Unidos, México, Chile, España, Bangladesh, India y Reino Unido.

Mis sueños

Estoy tan cansada
de la gente que nos llama soñadores
por todo lo que hicimos bien.

Tenemos tantos problemas: las emisiones,
y la tala,

o ambas cosas,

o comer las partes de animales que no necesitamos,

mientras se llenan los periódicos con las caras no tapadas
*Anónimo son siempre los mismos.

El río está hecho de deshechos,
el desierto ya no es el Sáhara:

está en nuestras venas.

Hay una brisa en nuestra garganta

que desaparece lento.
Y la ciencia ya no puede más con nuestro desastre.

Un día soñar con lo que está bien va a ser tan humillante
que ya no nos van a llamar soñadores,
van a buscar nuevas formas de torturarnos.

My dreams

I am so sick
of people calling us dreamers
for all those things we did well.

There are so many issues: emissions,
cutting down trees,

or both,

or eating animal parts we have no need for,

while newspapers are bursting with exposed faces
*Anonymous always includes the same people.

The river is made up of waste materials,
the desert is no longer the Sahara:

it is flowing inside our veins.

In our throats, a breeze

slowly vanishing.
And Science can no longer cope with our disasters.

One day, dreaming about what is right will be so humiliating
that they will no longer say we are dreamers,
and instead they will find new ways of torturing us.

Cerrar nuestros ojos va a ser tan ilegal,
que no vamos a poder ir a ningún lugar,
ni siquiera con los ojos cerrados.

Nos vamos a ver como una especie de Cristo,

separándose de la astillada cruz:
seremos su premio.
Y nuestros sueños nos van a atravesar las manos
como clavos de oro,
pero la sangre no va a caer esta vez desde esa corona de espinas.

Algo más va a caer.

Algo invisible se derramará.

Pero quién quedará en pie
para sentirlo.

Narciso

Narciso
se
hunde
lento
Y resucita.
Entre
periodistas
desilusionados.

Shutting our eyes will be considered so unlawful
that we will be unable to go anywhere
even with our eyes shut.

We will appear as some kind of Christ,

detaching himself from the splintering cross:
we will be their prize.
And our dreams will skewer our hands
like golden spikes,
though this time no blood will ooze from that crown of thorns.

Something else is going to pour out.

Something invisible will spill.

But who will remain standing
to feel what is taking place.

Narciso

Narciso
sinks
slowly
And then resuscitates.
Among
disappointed
journalists.

Levanta sus pies

azules,
en el mañana.

Narciso junta los fragmentos.
Arma una luna nueva.

Los mitos son reflejos
calcinados.

Narciso

tiene mil
espejos.

Nada perece. Nada permanece.

Narciso
fuga entre
las alas

de un
rompecabezas
d e s a j u s t a d o.

Y esos niños ciegos no pueden armarlo.
Ese es el final. Oficial
o reciclado.

He lifts his blue

feet,
in days to come.

Narciso collects all remaining fragments.
He assembles a new moon.

Myths are nothing but burnt out
reflections.

Narciso

has a thousand
mirrors.

Nothing at all perishes. Nothing remains.

Narciso
fleeing between
the wings

of a
m u d d l e d
jigsaw puzzle.

And those blind kids cannot put it together.
That is the very end. Whether official
or recycled, it is the end.

The end, Narciso
murdered

Del narciso en diez
televisores
asesinado.

En una
noche
oscura

de ninfas
y bosques
no
identificados.

Mis vidrios

Tantos vidrios
nos separan
que tal vez
solo las piedras
puedan quebrar
nuestras distancias

on ten TV sets.

During a
dark
night

with nymphs
and woods
yet to be
identified.

My bits of glass

So many bits of glass
separate us
that maybe
only stones
can shatter
the distance between you and me

Mis ídolos

Les voy a contar el secreto de muchos artistas consagrados:
Algunos están demasiado deprimidos, demasiado locos,
demasiado blancos,
demasiado ricos,
demasiado egocéntricos.
Incluso demasiado pedófilos o demasiado dealers.
Todos lo saben, pero muchos los siguen consumiendo,
como parejas disfuncionales de un crimen secreto.

Lo siento –No sabía que estaban ahí,

No me crean lo que estoy escribiendo. No es cierto.
Los artistas son talentosos.

Si seguimos usando las palabras correctas.
Si seguimos elaborando discursos perfectos...

Nadie va a ver los cuerpos.
Las piedras en sus manos.
La furia de las moscas.

Voy a tomar esa maldita flor del invierno,
Se la voy a dar a ese nene del metro,
ese que me pide una moneda.

Él vio el disfraz.
Él sabe que esto es falso.
Él sabe.

My idols

I am going to tell you the secret of many renowned artists:
Some are far too depressed, much too mad,
they are too white,
too rich,
far too egocentric.
They are even too much of a paedophile or a dealer.
Everyone knows about them, but many still guzzle their work,
just like a dysfunctional couple sharing secret wrongdoings.

I am sorry – I did not know they were there,

Do not believe what I am writing. It is not true.
Artists are talented.

If we continue using the right words.
If we go on writing perfect speeches...

No one will see the dead bodies.
The stones they are holding in their hands.
The fury of flies.

I will take that damned winter flower
and give it to that youngster in the tube,
yes, the one who is asking me for a coin.

He saw the disguise.
He knew it was all false.
He knew.

Mi final

El final es el corazón de los versos.
Es el arte de bajar el volumen.
Si el espectáculo valió la pena,
deberías estar de alguna forma involucrado:
porque ahora somos amigos,
despidiéndonos.

Espero ser más que una hoja gris de la calle,
caída y pisada,
y a punto de dejar de ser visible en tu vida.

Esto es el final.
Adiós.

My ending

The ending is at the heart of a poem.
It is the art of turning down the volume.
If the show was worth it after all,
you should get involved in some way:
because we are now friends,
saying goodbye to each other.

I hope to be more than a grey leaf in the street,
sprawled on the ground and trampled on,
and about to disappear from your life.

This is the end.
Goodbye.

CARLOS SAPOCHNIK
(Argentina)

Carlos Sapochnik was born in Buenos Aires in 1944; in 1968 he emigrated to London. He has designed and illustrated posters and books for many British theatres and publishers. His work has been exhibited in the UK, France, Poland, Czechia, Finland, and Japan. He has published research studies (*Drawing from the sight of absence*, 2020; *Group Relations and other meditations*, 2021) and bilingual poetry with Alltogethernow Press (*So far so good*, 2018; *Drawing strength*, 2019; *Wear & Tear*, 2021; *Half a silence again*, 2022). More recently, he writes poetry simultaneously in Castilian and English, with accompanying illustrations.

*Carlos Sapochnik nació en Buenos Aires en 1944; y emigró a Londres en 1968. Ha diseñado e ilustrado posters y libros para numerosos teatros y editoriales británicas. Sus diseños y dibujos han sido expuestos en Gran Bretaña, Francia, Polonia, Czechia, Finlandia, y Japón. Ha publicado estudios de investigación (*Drawing from the sight of absence, *2020;* Group Relations and other meditations, *2021) y libros de poesía bilingüe con la Alltogethernow Press (*So far so good, *2018;* Drawing strength, *2019;* Wear & Tear, *2021). Últimamente elabora su poesía simultáneamente en castellano, inglés, y dibujando.*

cuando volví de Troya harto
de viajes y peleas por
ciudades mujeres brocados
calderos aplastando
guerreros sin sangre dentro
de caparazones de bronce su
horrenda forma adornada
con pequeños pies de
crustáceo desmesuradas
garras los ojos ciegos
escudos endurecidos
protegiendo la blanca carne
oliendo a lunas en cuarto
menguante creciente y su
cambiante gibosidad ahora
solo estoy de paso apenas
me miran ignoran que aún
tengo superpoderes

when I returned from Troy sick and tired of
travelling and fighting for
cities women brocades
cauldrons
crushing warriors with no blood within
their bronze shells their
horrid figures embellished
with tiny crustacean feet
overgrown claws
blind eyes
hardened shields
protecting their white flesh
smelling of moons in their first quarter and
waxing crescents
and their mutable
hump-shape
now that I am just passing by, they
barely look at me, ignoring the fact that I still
have superpowers

de noche los dedos se
hinchan alargan los pies
más allá del ropero alguien
llora hasta anegar piso
cortinas la puerta celeste de
metal y vidrio flota hacia
futuros inciertos donde todo
se agranda lentamente una
nube de algodón crece hasta
llenarle la garganta cuánto
más tranquilo callado
despierto en su cama de
niño rozando apenas el lomo
de sus libros de aventuras
sobre el estante en la
oscuridad interrumpida por
ruidos y destellos de
esporádicos tranvías la
respiración de su hermanito
uno que otro grito ahogado
durante la pendencia en la
habitación contigua la
pared delicadamente
transparente casi veía lo que
hacían aunque por la
mañana pretendieran que
había pasado nada lo podía
engañar

at night-time
fingers swell, feet lengthen
beyond the wardrobe someone
weeps until they flood the floor
the curtains the sky-blue metal and
glass door floating towards
uncertain futures where all things
slowly enlarge
a cotton-wool cloud expands
until it fills his throat, the
more peaceful he is
the more quiet
awake in his childhood bed
barely skimming the spine of his
adventure books
on the shelf in the midst
of a darkness disrupted
by the noises and flickers
of occasional trams his
little brother's breathing
the odd stifled scream
during the brawl
in the adjoining room the
wall of which was so delicately transparent
that he could almost see what
they were doing even though
in the morning they pretended
nothing had happened yet nothing
would deceive him

cómo ha venido a parar tan
lejos de su abuelita y el
diminuto departamento en
el barrio judío la pequeña
cocina banco de madera
celeste pringoso mantel de
hule aquí es distinta la
música el idioma que habla
escucha la niebla sobre
pajaritos libros y casas tan
bajas ahora distantes los
edificios altos caballos
tranvías un deslumbrante
bandoneón por la ventana
del bar dónde la piel era más
oscura y el pelo negro
brillante caluroso cielo azul
se puso tan frío de niño
había visto en el cine un
buen hombre dormirse
perdido en la nieve no volvió
a despertar dijo Valéry el
poema nunca se termina
solo se abandona

how is it that he ended up so very far away
from dear granny and the tiny apartment
in the Jewish quarter the small
kitchen the wooden bench
the greasy blue oilcloth covering the table
over here it is all different
the music the language he speaks
and he listens to the fog
above those little birds, books, such low-built
houses
now that tall buildings are so far away
horses trams a dazzling bandoneon
through the window of that bar
where skin was darker and black hair
shone a warm blue sky and
he would get so cold as a child
and in the cinema he saw
a good man falling asleep
lost in the snow
and never waking up Valéry
said that a poem
is never finished
only abandoned

mira lo que ha escrito no
entiende los garabatos
semejantes a los de su
abuelo contaba cosas
pasadas cuando imigrante
de Moldova escribía poco en
tinta azul con letra grande y
agitada qué pensaba aquél
corpulento hombre sombrío
enormes orejas cejas espesas
sus pies bailoteando sentado
inmóvil en el sillón del living
tan callado hubiera querido
hablar con él conocer su
historia una vez relató de
muchacho tuvo que escapar
con su amigo de noche por la
montaña la nieve sin
zapatos pies envueltos en
trapos ensangrentados
mientras cosacos mataban
judíos a tiros y sablazos su
amigo fue herido en una
mano por una bala perdida
le arrancó los dedos con
frecuencia repetía divertido
cuando eras un nene quisiste
sacarle una foto a un perro
le pediste al perro que sonría

looking at what he has written
he does not understand
the scribbles so alike those of
his grandfather
who would tell stories from the past
when he was an immigrant
from Moldova he did not write much
in blue ink with large and frantic characters
what did that burly and gloomy man
think with huge ears heavy eyebrows
his feet twirling in a dance when he was sitting down
immobile
in the living-room armchair
so quiet he would have
wanted to speak to him
and find out about his past
he once told the story of when, as a young boy,
he had to flee with his friend at night
through mountains
the snow
with no shoes
their feet wrapped in blood-spattered
rags while Cossacks
killed Jews
shooting at them, slashing them
with sabres and his
friend was injured
a stray bullet tore off the fingers in his hand
and he would repeatedly say
in amusement when you were a child
you wanted to take a picture of a dog
and you asked the dog to smile

cuánto más amable es su
almohada que la mía
cuando deslizo la cabeza
entre su hombro tibio y el
colchón huele a cucha
mientras no percibe la
planchada funda tan
fresquita aunque dormida
gruña date vuelta
interrumpiendo mi
ronquido de alimaña
disputando con furia la
frazada que suelo apropiar
en nuestra nocturna
escaramuza por la vida no se
me escapan sus dulces
detalles que persisten pese a
la avanzada edad las
repeticiones de penas
placeres olvidos hijos casas
países epidemias a través de
la gastada complejidad del
ancho mundo

how much gentler her pillow
is than mine as
I slide my head
between her warm shoulder
and the mattress smelling like a hutch
while
she does not feel the fresh and ironed
pillowcase and even asleep
she snarls at me to turn
in the bed so that I stop
my beastly snoring
both of us fiercely competing for the blanket
it is usually me who takes possession of it
in our nightly skirmishes
through life
always aware as I am of
her sweet subtleties
persisting despite advanced age
and repetitions of sorrows
pleasures
things forgotten
children houses countries epidemics
throughout the worn-out complexities
of this vast world

comenzó a vender o regalar
todos sus libros anticipando
llegará el final dijo no
quedará nada nadie sabe
nadie puede saber mi
infinita contricción y
cansancio ha leído recuerda
esta frase su discurso un
museo de citas y textos ha
pensado algo suyo pocas
veces repite lo que entiende
en sus dos idiomas hablan
discuten entre si mientras él
obediente anota fervoroso
escribiente de esa voz sin
aliento escuchada tan cerca
la lengua materna le besa la
boca al hablar

he began to sell or give away
all of his books anticipating what
was to come
the end would be here he said
nothing will remain nobody
knows
nobody
can know my infinite
remorse and
my tiredness
he has read and remembers
that phrase his speech a museum
of quotes and texts
he has seldom thought of something
belonging to him
he repeats what he
understands in his two languages
for they both talk
argue between them whilst he
obediently
zealously takes notes
a scribe of a voice with no breath
heard ever so closely
his mother-tongue kisses
his mouth when he speaks

JUAN TOLEDO
(Colombia)

Juan Toledo is a translator, podcaster, editor and teacher. He was born in Bogotá. He studied Chemistry at Universidad Nacional and then Literature and Philosophy at Birkbeck College, UCL, where he also acquired an MA in Translation and Hispanic Studies. He has lived in London for over three decades, and for over two decades he was a cultural administrator within the Arts Division of the British Council. For three years he was the editor of *Crónica Latina*, one of the first newspapers to be published in Castilian in the UK, and later on he was the director of a broadcasting station in Brixton, South London. In 2020 he published his poetry collection *Ocurrencias y recurrencias*. At present, he is the editor and co-presenter of *Artefacto* and *The Programme*, two *ZTR Radio* podcasts. He is also editor of the digital cultural magazine *Perro Negro*, which is published bilingually.

Juan Toledo es traductor, podcaster, editor y profesor. Nació en Bogotá, estudió química en la Universidad Nacional y luego literatura y filosofía en Birkbeck College, UCL, donde también completó una maestría en traducción y estudios hispánicos. Ha residido en la capital británica por más de seis lustros y por un poco más de dos décadas laboró como gestor cultural en la Arts Division del British Council del Reino Unido. Por tres años editó uno de los primeros periódicos en castellano del Reino Unido, Crónica Latina *y años más tarde fue director de una emisora de radio independiente en Brixton, en el sur de Londres. Publicó* Ocurrencias y recurrencias *(2020). Actualmente es editor y co-presentador de* Artefacto *y* The Programme *dos podcasts de ZTR Radio y editor de la revista cultural bilingüe digital Perro Negro.*

Intemperie

Ha sido en vano
pues bien sé
que la lluvia y el viento
borrarán mi nombre escrito
en el muro de tu memoria.

Empiricismo

La mano que acaricia tu rostro

no es mi mano.
Los labios que besan tus hombros y tu cuello
no son mis labios.
No soy el amante atento
si no la bestia urgida
sin causa o efecto
trastabillando en ese tiempo fragmentado
que es la felicidad.

Retorno

He regresado a un lugar donde nunca he estado.
He regresado otro
y es otro a lo que he regresado.
He regresado en busca de ella.
He regresado a despojarla de todo,
de todo aquello que no se llevó la nada.

The elements

It has all been in vain
for I know well
that the rain and the wind
will erase my name
written on the walls of your memory.

Empiricism

The hand that caresses your face

is not my hand.
The lips kissing your shoulders and your neck
are not my lips.

I am not the attentive lover
but the hurrying beast
with no cause nor effect
stumbling in that fragmented timeline
called happiness.

Homecoming

I have returned to a place where I had never been before.
I have returned as someone else
and to what I have returned is
something else too.
I have returned looking for her.
I have returned to deprive her of everything,
of all those things that nothingness did not take away.

Pornografía

Tanta y tan variada belleza

tan lasciva y solícita
con alguien como yo.

Amor onanista, puro, sin reproches,
mudo, íntimo y virtual.
Imagen convertida en acto,
acto de amor que es solo
la oquedad del acto.
El acto de un acto.
Espejismo de un placer
huero y jadeante.

Transacciones

Todo amor es una transacción,
cada deseo un trueque,
perdonar es un empeño.
El olvido, una factura perdida.
La nostalgia, una cuenta sin pagar.

La desdicha es
no haber pagado a tiempo
la valía de lo que valía
a cambio
mendigamos dichosos
esa moneda corriente

Pornography

So much and so assorted all this beauty

so lascivious and solicitous
towards someone like me.

Onanist love, without a single rebuke,
speechless, intimate and virtual.
An image spun into an act,
an act of love that is only
the hollowness of an act.
The act of an act.
A mirage of pleasure
vacuous and panting.

Transactions

All love is a transaction,
every desire signifies bartering,
forgiving is an endeavour.
Forgetting, but an invoice that is lost.
Nostalgia, a bill that must be settled.

Wretchedness means
not having paid on time
the value of what it was valued at
and in exchange we
blissfully beg
for that common coinage

que es el afecto de la gente
para luego urdir
nuestra propia estafa
al no saber qué cueste más:
si la ofrenda virginal
frente al altar
o la promesa jadeante en el lecho
aún por saldar.

Lenguaraces

Santo Tomás de Aquino: 8 millones de palabras
Aristóteles: un millón
Platón: medio millón
Sócrates: muchas
Wittgenstein: "De lo que no se puede hablar, es mejor callarse."
Mi madre: "Silencio, estoy viendo mi telenovela."

which is the affection of others
and later on we concoct
our own fraud
since we do not know which is the more valuable:
whether the virginal offer
in front of the altar
or the panting promise on the bridal bed
yet to be paid off.

Loose-tongued

Saint Thomas Aquinas: eight million words
Aristotle: one million
Plato: half a million
Socrates: many
Wittgenstein: " Whereof one cannot speak, thereof one must be silent."
My mother: "Keep quiet! I'm watching my soap opera on TV."

Anaximandro

De donde las cosas
se han originado
pasan nuevamente
a otra cosa,
es el orden.

Se realizan
la reparación y la compensación
por sus injusticias
conforme
al orden de los tiempos

Justicia cósmica o
justicia humana,
religión
o filosofía

¿No son esas cosas
tan sólo
el deseo perenne
de ordenar
ese desorden emocional
de nuestro existir?

Anaximander

From where things
originate
they move on
to become something else,
that is the order of things.

Both reparation and remuneration
are carried out
because of the wrongs committed
according
to the order of the ages.

Cosmic justice or
human justice,
religion
or philosophy

Are all these nothing
but the perennial wish
to put some order into
the emotional disorder
of our existence?

Fama

Tuvo el merecido pero
miserable honor
de ser el autor más
importante en un país
donde no se leía.

Analfabetismo:
veintitrés por ciento.
Analfabetismo literario:
setenta y tres por ciento
Tiraje de un nuevo libro
doscientos cincuenta ejemplares.
Valor promedio de un libro:
tres días y medio de salario mínimo.

Su reducido pero
ilustre público estaba
conformado por unos
contados estudiantes del
Liceo San Ignacio de Loyola,
las hijas gemelas
del embajador japonés,
el rector del Alma Mater,
El subjefe de los servicios
de inteligencia del Estado,
el ministro de agricultura
y el hijo bohemio del
embajador de su país
en París.

Fame

He had the well-deserved yet
miserable honour
of being the most important author
in a country where people
did not read.

Illiteracy:
Twenty-three per cent.
Literary illiteracy:
Seventy-three per cent
Print-run of a new book:
Two hundred and fifty copies.
Average value of a book:
Three and a half days of the minimum wage.

Though limited in number,
his illustrious readers
included a number of
students from the
Liceo San Ignacio de Loyola,
the twin daughters
of the Japanese ambassador,
the rector of his *Alma Mater*,
the deputy head of the Intelligence
Services of the State,
the Secretary for Agriculture,
and the bohemian son of his country's
ambassador in Paris.

Así que sus libros
fueron más comentados
que leídos. Muchas páginas
y pasajes de los dos volúmenes
de su Obras Completas *y el*
subsecuente magnum opus
en verso
Memorias de un mudo
pasaron a ser contadas,
recontadas, cantadas
y tergiversadas en
no pocos casos
con nuevos personajes
y desenlaces nunca descritos.

Por eso el arzobispo,
quien tampoco lo había leído,
atinó perfectamente cuando
en la misa de requiem
en la catedral mayor, con
el féretro cubierto con
el pabellón nacional,
unas flores y tres libros
lo llamó: "Nuestro Homero"

And so, his books
were more commented on
than read. And many of the pages
and excerpts from the two volumes
of his Complete Works and the later
magnum opus
in verse and with the title of
Memorias de un mudo
would be told as stories,
retold, sung
and misrepresented in no few
cases
with new characters
and never previously described
denouements.

This is the reason why the Archbishop,
who had not read his works either,
got it perfectly right when,
during the requiem mass
that took place in the main cathedral, standing
in front of the coffin draped with the national flag,
a number of flowers and three of his books,
called him: "Our very own Homer"

ENRIQUE D. ZATTARA
(Argentina)

Enrique D. Zattara was born in Venado Tuerto (Argentina) in 1954. He lived in Rosario and Buenos Aires until 1992; then in Málaga, Spain until 2014; he currently lives in London. He has a degree in Philosophy from UNED in Madrid. He is a writer, literary critic and journalist, and has been a correspondent and editor for several newspapers in both Argentina and Spain. He is also the founder of a number of literary magazines: *Arte Nova* and *Contrapelo* (Buenos Aires), and *Utopía Poética* and *Letras Axárquicas* (Spain). He has published seven poetry collections, two novels and two short-story collections, and another nine books in several genres. He is the director of the multimedia cultural project El Ojo de la Cultura Hispanoamericana. He also coordinates several writing workshops, as well as the Club de Lectura at the Instituto Cervantes in London.

Enrique D. Zattara nació en 1954 en Venado Tuerto (Argentina), y ha vivido en Rosario y Buenos Aires (hasta 1992), en Málaga, España (hasta 2014) y actualmente en Londres (UK). Graduado en Filosofía por la UNED de Madrid, escritor, crítico literario y periodista, ha sido corresponsal y director de diversos periódicos en Argentina y España, y fundador de varias revistas literarias: Arte Nova y Contrapelo *(Buenos Aires),* Utopía Poética y Letras Axárquicas *(España). Publicó siete libros de poesía, dos novelas, dos libros de relatos, y nueve más en diversos géneros.*
Es Director del proyecto cultural multimedia El Ojo de la Cultura Hispanoamericana. Coordina Talleres de Escritura y el Club de Lectura del Instituto Cervantes de Londres.

El desierto

Quizá esté en el momento en que vivir es
errar en completa soledad al fondo de un
momento ilimitado, en que la luz
no cambia y todos los residuos se parecen
Samuel Beckett, "Malone muere"

En Sbá la muerte tiene un tono
que rueda al vacío desde arpegios convulsos,
un tono callado como el viento que modifica el paisaje.

Sólo la muerte, sin embargo,
cambia algo. Ya no hay paisaje, no hay
punto de vista desde donde ejecutar la música.

Hasta tanto, sólo el viento:
feroz simún o la calma brisa de ciertas horas
y el sol de plomo sobre el ereg desierto.
Cuando cambia el paisaje:
aquí y allá crecen y se derrumban dunas estriadas
como el fantasmal vaivén de un mar en cámara lenta.

A veces, una caravana atraviesa la aridez
dejando leves huellas que se borran a su paso.
Los hombres se detienen, hacen fuego,
elevan las plegarias a sus dioses.
Al cabo, demasiado rápido, retorna el silencio.

El viento no corroe:
sólo mueve de aquí para allá las arenas gualdas,
como nieve de oro sibilante.

The desert

And perhaps he has come to that stage of his instant when to live is
to wander the last of the living in the depths of an instant
without bounds, where the light never changes
and the wrecks look all alike.
Samuel Beckett, 'Malone dies'

In Sbá, death acquires a tone that
swirls towards the abyss from winding arpeggios,
a tone as quiet as the wind that alters the landscape.

Only death, however,
changes things. There is no landscape any longer, and no
viewpoint from which to perform music.

For now, only the wind:
a fierce simoon or the calming breeze during certain hours
and a scorching sun over the Erg desert.
And when the landscape changes:
here and there ribbed dunes swell and break apart
like the ghostly sway of a sea in slow motion.

At times, a caravan crosses the parchedness
leaving behind dim traces that fade in its path.
Men come to a stop, light a fire,
raise prayers to their gods.
And after a while, though far too swiftly, silence returns.

The wind will not erode:
it solely displaces the gilded sands from here to there,
like snow of hissing gold.

Hasta que el momento llega.
Sólo sabemos que por fin la música ha cesado.
Ignoramos si es apenas un compás vacío
detrás del cual se abre
simplemente
               un nuevo paisaje inmóvil.

Hora cero

Puede que sea un punto de partida:
nunca creí en la existencia de los padres.
Un padre es alguien que ocupa la silla de la cabecera
(cuando el televisor está apagado).
Un padre es alguien que lo ignora todo de las cosas.
Padre es quien funda
la tragedia irreparable de la vida:
tu familia.
Padre no hay ninguno:
es sólo una señal sobre la frente.

Puede que sea ese el principio del camino.
Después, un hombre se sienta
a contemplar su soledad por la ventana,
abrumado por la perfecta crueldad del universo.
Se palpa la camisa,
hace gestos al espejo.
Trata de ser cordial y ni siquiera puede.

El fantasma del rey Hamlet está donde todo empieza,
y siempre sospecharemos que Gertrudis
asoma detrás de cada asesinato.

And all of this is taking place until the moment arrives.
We only know that music has finally ceased.
What we do not know is whether what we hear is
barely an empty beat
behind which
a fresh motionless landscape

$$\text{unravels.}$$

Zero hour

It may be a point of departure:
I never believed in the existence of parents.
A father is someone who sits at the head of the table
(assuming the TV is switched off).
A father is someone who ignores everything about things.
What is a father but the founder
of the irreparable tragedy of a life:
in other words, your family.
Father, there is none:
he is nothing but a sign on your forehead.

Maybe that is the start of the path.
And after that, a man sits down
to behold his solitude through the window,
overwhelmed as he is by the universe's perfect cruelty.
He feels his shirt
and gesticulates in front of the mirror.
He tries to be friendly, but he is not even capable of that.

The ghost of King Hamlet is where it all begins,
and we shall always suspect that Gertrude
was behind every single murder.

Mi primo era un gigante vestido de blanco

¿No existe acaso -en la noche silenciosa-
un agujero azul por donde comienzan los caminos hacia el mundo?
Sueño más alto aun que todo lo que se ha escrito:
ver el mar allende las colinas
y un arrebujo de nieve en la cima de los picos solitarios.

Así es como empieza la fiebre:
pensamos en conocer lugares
con extraños nombres como Ekland o Miranao.
Sitios como los rincones más secretos
del cuerpo de una mujer que amamos
con el furor del amor que solo guarda un hombre joven.

Pueblos pequeños encalados como gemas blancas en los cerros;
mares inmensos que agotan los más rudos corazones;
auroras amarillas suspendidas en la quietud de una laguna;
noches de lujuria y alcohol al pie de rascacielos:
¿qué hay en el mundo que no esté ya en nuestros sueños?

Pero no basta:
somos héroes antiguos necesitados de aventura,
vestigios de algún nómade pasado,
argonautas eternamente insatisfechos.
Un atardecer subimos en silencio a un tren sin pasaje de retorno
y el presente nos devela apenas detenidos,
pasajeros en estaciones donde
esperamos
           sólo algún
                    cambio de vías.

My cousin was a giant in a white suit

Is there not by any chance -in the silence of the night-
a blue pit where all routes towards the world come into being?
My dreams travel so much further than all that has been written:
seeing the sea beyond the hills
and snow entangled on the cusp of solitary peaks.

That is how fever starts:
we yearn to know places
with strange names like Eklund or Miranao.
Places like the most secret recesses
of the body of the woman we love
with the rapturous love that only a young man can possess.

Lowly, whitewashed villages like white gemstones along hills;
vast seas that expend the coarsest of hearts;
yellow dawns dangling in the stillness of a lagoon;
nights of lust and booze at the foot of skyscrapers:
what is there in the world not already in our dreams?

But this is not enough:
we are ancient heroes in need of adventure,
vestiges of some long-gone nomad,
eternally dissatisfied argonauts.
It happened that one day long ago at dusk we silently boarded
a train without a return ticket,
the present time revealing that we are hardly delayed in our journey,
passengers we are in stations
 where we await
                    solely for
                              some switch on the track.

Cuerpo velado

La luz dorada que se filtra entre los listones de madera.
El aura de luz que nimba los listones de la persiana veneciana.
El breve chorro luminoso que chispea en las aristas de la cama.
El chorro de luz reflejado que se agolpa en la mano que cuelga al borde de la cama.
Las hebras de luz que se confunden en la cobriza mata de tu pelo.
La prolija alternancia de luz y sombra que fabrica listones
rayando la dorada superficie de tu cuerpo desnudo,
la mata cobriza de tu pelo,
tu mano que cuelga al borde de la cama.

La perentoria llamada de esa persiana veneciana
que arrastra en sus imprevistos listones de sombra
la luz incierta de una mañana silenciosa,
de una cama revuelta por los ritos del amor,
de un cuerpo dormido
que hace tiempo sólo ocupa sitio en la memoria.

El yo poético pierde el hilo de la historia

¿A quién habla Foucault con energía vigorosa?
Megáfono en las manos: firme gesto de batalla.
Cámaras y micrófonos sobrevolando las cabezas de la gente.
¿Qué decía Foucault aquella tarde?
Y a su lado, ¿qué piensa Jean Paul Sartre?
Al fondo de la escena la instantánea muestra
la geometría monótona de una nave industrial como cualquiera otra.

A veiled body

Golden light seeps through the wooden slats.
An aura of light haloes the laths of the Venetian blind.
A brief rush of light sparkles on the edges of the bed.
That rush of reflected light gathers on a hand dangling from the side of the bed.
The strands of light mingle with the coppery clumps of your hair.
The painstaking shifts of light and shadow producing slats
scuffing the golden surface of your naked body,
the coppery clumps of your hair,
your hand dangling from the side of the bed.

The insistent tapping produced by that Venetian blind
that drags, with its unpredicted slats of shade,
the uncertain light of a silent morning, of
a bed dishevelled by the rites of love, of
someone fast asleep
who, for some time now, occupies only a place in our memory.

The poetic self loses the thread of History

So, who is Foucault talking to with such vigorous energy?
In his hands, a megaphone: firmly in readiness for battle.
Cameras and microphones hovering over people's heads.
What was Foucault saying that afternoon?
And alongside him, what did Jean Paul Sartre think?
In the background, the snapshot shows
the monotonous geometry of an industrial plant just like any other.

Albertito traza con el dedo
una línea invisible entre dos ángulos: desde el ángulo inferior, sobre la izquierda,
hasta el superior, a la derecha. El idéntico camino
que la mirada del fotógrafo propone.
Traza una línea oblicua con el dedo
mientras el megáfono de Foucault se desliza
por debajo de la yema un poco húmeda (hace calor esta tarde)
del dedo de Albertito.

Las fotos están allí, sobre el tablero.
Esparcidas sobre el tablero de metal del escritorio
en el silencio de la redacción vacía.
¿Qué hace Albertito, por cierto,
a esta hora en la redacción vacía?
La redacción donde alguien olvidó devolver a los cajones
una pila de fotos que ahora él está mirando,
mirando cómo Foucault y Sartre arengan a la gente
frente a la geometría monótona de una nave industrial como cualquiera otra.
¿El destino azaroso lo condujo hacia estas fotos?
Puede también que sólo haya sido, claro,
que está haciendo tiempo hasta la hora de la cita con su novia
(los caminos de dios son inescrutables).

Lo que nadie va a poner en duda, sin embargo,
es que las fotos están allí, sobre el tablero:
la foto en la que Sartre y Foucault arengan a la gente
con un megáfono frente a una nave industrial como cualquiera otra.
Y ahora Albertito – por azar o por destino –
pasa su dedo sobre ella y la contempla: hay algo que lo inquieta
y quizás hasta haya empezado a olvidar la cita con su novia.
Se pregunta, insistentemente: ¿por qué ocurre que él esté allí ahora mismo,
y por qué alguien olvidó devolver las fotos a la cajonera?

Albertito traces with his finger
an invisible line between two angles: from the lower angle, on the left,
to the upper one, on the right. Thus, it is the same route
as projected by the gaze of the photographer.
He traces an oblique line with his finger
whilst Foucault's megaphone slides
under Albertito's slightly damp fingertip (it is a warm afternoon, after all).

The photographs are there, on the tabletop.
Scattered on the metal tabletop of the desk
in the silence of the empty newsroom.
Incidentally, what is Albertito doing, at that time,
in the empty newsroom?
It is the same newsroom where someone forgot to place the pictures
                              [back in the drawer where they were kept,
He is now looking at that pile of pictures,
seeing how Foucault and Sartre harangue people
against the monotonous geometry of an industrial plant just like any other.
Was it nothing but haphazard destiny leading him towards those photographs?
It could well have been, of course, that
he was killing time until he met up with his girlfriend for their date
(the ways of god are unfathomable).

What no one will doubt, however,
is that the pictures are there, on the tabletop:
the photograph in which Sartre and Foucault harangue people
with a megaphone, in front of an industrial plant just like any other.
And now Albertito –whether because of chance or destiny–
slides his finger over the image and looks ever so carefully
at it; there is something there that makes him feel uneasy
and it could be that he is beginning to forget about the date he has
                              [with his girlfriend.

El Yo Poético sin embargo, se hace preguntas más sesudas:
¿por qué estaban allí Sartre y Foucault aquella tarde,
arengando a la gente frente a una nave industrial como cualquiera otra?
¿la guerra de Argelia? ¿una huelga de obreros de Renault?
¿denunciar la injusticia del sistema carcelario?
No se sabe: los epígrafes se han perdido
y la memoria de Albertito no registra tan efímero detalle.
¿Y entonces, la foto, de qué habla?
interroga – filosófico - el tozudo Yo Poético.
¿Quizás del gesto enérgico de Foucault,
de la ancianidad serena de aquel Sartre?
¿Qué es, en definitiva, lo que importa?
            ¿En qué consiste el hilo de la historia?

Albertito, por su parte, ya ha perdido el hilo de la historia:
a él le importa, verdaderamente, descubrir qué lo ha traído a esta hora
hasta el silencio de la redacción vacía
y cómo es que se ha olvidado de la cita con su novia.

He insistently asks himself: why is it that he is there now, at that precise moment,
and why did someone forget to put the pictures back in the drawer?

And yet the poetic self asks more judicious questions:
Why were Sartre and Foucault there that afternoon,
haranguing people in front of an industrial plant like any other?
The Algerian war? a strike by workers at the Renault plant?
protesting against the injustices of the prison system?
No one knows: the captions to the photographs were lost
and Albertito's memory cannot register such fleeting detail.
And so, what is the photograph talking about?
That is the question that the stubborn poetic self philosophically asks.
Is it possibly talking about Foucault's assertive gesture,
or about the serene old age in the case of Sartre?
What matters, ultimately?
                What does the thread of history entail exactly?

Albertito, on his part, has already lost the thread of history:
what he really cares about is to find out what brought him at this hour
all the way to the silence of an empty newsroom
and why it is that he has forgotten about the date he had with his girlfriend.

Godot

La caña del pescador
se tiende como una esperanza hacia el mar.
Su débil apariencia cimbrea igual que un asta
inexplicable.
Nadie ve el hilo tenso sobre las ondas,
solo el pescador aguarda:
él puede ver lo invisible y espera.
Ya habrá el débil tirón,
el súbito arquearse de la caña,
el vértice superior acercándose a las olas
en una sed que no podrá saciarse.

Pero en esta marina repetida
no debe olvidarse que es posible
que la línea no encuentre resistencia:
que su alerta tensión permanezca sin respuesta,
que apenas el aire incesante pulse su nota monocorde.

Godot

Towards the sea itself
a fisherman's rod
outspreading like an expectation.
Its frail structure quivers as an
inexplicable antler.
No one can see the tense thread over undulations,
it is only the fisherman who is expectant:
he can see that which is invisible, and so he looks out.
A weak jerk will materialise,
the sudden arching of the rod,
with the apex drawing near the waves like
a thirst that cannot be quenched.

But in this reiterating seascape
we must not forget that it could be that
the fishing line encounters no resistance:
that its watchful tension remains unanswered,
with the incessant wind barely plucking its single-stringed note.

INDEX

Ilustration Index

Printed in Great Britain
by Amazon